500 Years Later

500 Years Later

An Oral History of Final Fantasy VII

Matt Leone

Foreword by Hironobu Sakaguchi
With 16 illustrations

500 Years Later
Contents

Foreword

A

By Hironobu Sakaguchi

When I think back to making *Final Fantasy VII*, three moments come to mind.

The first happened before we started developing the game itself. We formed a small team to make a tech demo of what *Final Fantasy* could look like running on high-end Silicon Graphics hardware. I've talked about this a lot over the years, but seeing that come alive was something special. It's not just that I was surprised or blown away by it, which I was, but it took away any doubts I had. Instantly, I knew we needed to move forward and make a game that looked like that. That was a defining moment in the process – getting that feeling of 'we need to do this'.

The second came once we started working on the game itself. We had hired Motonori Sakakibara, who came from a computer graphics background, to work on the game's cutscenes. At one point I gave him a vague direction for the game's opening sequence – just a sentence or so description of how the camera could zoom out from Midgar to show the city's scale and kick off the story. With that, he went to work and came up with a scene that still impresses me. When I saw what he made – with music from our composer Nobuo Uematsu layered on top – it seemed like everything was coming together. It felt bold.

I'll never forget seeing that. I knew we couldn't turn back.

Then the third came right before we finished work on the game. We put together a playable demo that we released to the public, and in the final scene of that demo we showed an explosion in Midgar. I felt we had something very impressive with that, and I figured it made for a great way to end the demo, to really show off the game's graphics. At that point, we were almost done with development and I was happy with what we had. I just hoped fans would feel the same way.

As it turned out, many did and the game ended up selling pretty well.

It's funny, though. I try not to dwell too much on the past. If I think back hard on *FFVII*, I'll remember certain aspects that I'm not perfectly happy with.

For example, at the time, I had a clear theme that I wanted to communicate about what happens after you die, and what that means. This wasn't only in *FFVII* but *Final Fantasy: The Spirits Within* as well, so obviously it meant a lot to me. I had this idea and I really wanted people to just, please, understand what it all meant. So I sort of directly injected that into the game and film.

Now, looking back many years later, I feel like – even though I was an adult at the time – I wasn't mature enough to tell that story in such a direct way. I'm almost embarrassed today to think that I did that.

But I try not to worry about that too much.

Over my career, I've found that if I keep thinking about a game once it's done, or keep second guessing my choices and stay inside that world, I kind of get eaten up by my creation. That makes it much more difficult to move on to the next project. Whenever I finish a game, I feel like I have to let it go. It's hard but, at a certain point, I need to do that.

So when I think of *FFVII* now, I think of it as something I've passed on to the fans. I think it's great that, after we finished the game, we were able to hand it over and essentially let it take on a second life with their theories and speculation.

Over the past 20 years, I've heard from players around the world who love the game, and it means a lot whenever they mention their favourite aspects or parts of the story. It reminds me of how I feel about games that have a special place in my heart.

It feels great that it's out there for fans and, if they can cherish those memories and have an emotional connection with the title and save a special place in their hearts for it, then that's all I can really ask for.

Prologue

1

Nobuo Uematsu

'We treated it like a hobby, not a career. We just
wanted to do what we liked. We weren't worried
about our salaries or living situations or thinking, "Where is this company going?"'

Today, it sits above a Doutor coffee shop a few doors from a train station in a busy part of Hiyoshi, Yokohama.

Visit the building and you won't see a plaque commemorating the history or remnants of a company whose characters went on to model Louis Vuitton clothes and sell millions of games. Yet on that spot in 1983, inside his father's office space, founder Masafumi Miyamoto began a development studio called Square.

Initially, it wasn't even a formally designated company. It was a room where people came and went as they pleased, like a club or an after-school programme.

Some describe the company in its early days as a family

business. One of Square's first hires, Shinichiro Kajitani, joined simply because he was friends with Miyamoto. Another, Hironobu Sakaguchi, designed games while working part time.

'We treated it like a hobby, not a career,' says longtime Square composer Nobuo Uematsu. 'We just wanted to do what we liked. We weren't worried about our salaries or living situations or thinking, "Where is this company going?"'

But, as often tends to happen, people grow up and things change.

After a few early successes and stumbles, Square found a hit in the *Final Fantasy* role-playing game series. Moved into progressively larger offices. Hired hundreds of people. Built a portfolio.

'Eventually, Square's stock went public, and Sakaguchi-san and people on the management side had to focus hard on the financial goals they had to reach, the unit numbers that they had to hit,' says Uematsu.

'That whole mentality started to change around the time of *Final Fantasy VII.*'

When *FFVII* shipped in 1997, it was Square's cash cow. The game pioneered 3D graphics techniques, helped Sony's PlayStation outperform its competitors, established Japanese RPGs in the West and went on to sell more than 11 million copies. To many fans, it defined Square as a company.

Team members describe it as a perfect storm – Square still

acted like a small company but had the resources of a big one, and was willing to pour its money into one of the game industry's most ambitious projects right as the 3D graphics industry was beginning to take off.

'I don't think I've felt that kind of excitement ever since,' says programmer Hiroshi Kawai. 'It wasn't just the fact that Square had the resources to get all the people and the hardware and the technology together but, even before seeing anything run, it was as if we knew we were going to be making history.'

In late 2014, I started researching this story for the website Polygon.

It started as a small solo

project, just to see what might
be possible, and ended up taking
more than three years with
help from over 20 people. We
conducted dozens of interviews
and photoshoots around the
world, partnered with a game
design school to make an online
trivia game, designed a custom
layout for the online version
of the story, filmed and edited
a handful of short documentaries,
and generally said 'yes' whenever
a new idea came along.

It became the story that just
wouldn't die.

And now, for the final step in
that process, we've turned it into
the book you're holding. It has
taken a long time to get to this
point, but working on this project

has been one of the highlights of my career.

Ahead, in the words of more than 30 people who had hands in the original game, you'll find a story about a company in transition – and the money, politics and talent that pushed it over the edge.

Origins

2

2.1
The man behind *Final Fantasy*

Without Hironobu Sakaguchi, Square might have folded early on.

In the mid-'80s, shortly after Square started out, the company was still finding its footing in the game industry. It had developed a string of modestly successful PC titles but, when Nintendo's Famicom console came along in Japan (known as the Nintendo Entertainment System in the West), Square decided to gamble heavily on the new machine. It showered the console with games, hoping to see strong returns. But, initially, they didn't come. The team ran low on money and showed signs it might fold.

When Square's first *Final Fantasy* game hit the Famicom in 1987, that luck started to change. Thanks to an elaborate story and high-end production values, the series went on to become one of the biggest successes on Nintendo's console – and then its successor, the Super Famicom. In the late '80s, the series pulled Square out of financial trouble. By the '90s, it was the rocket almost everyone at the company grabbed onto.

For *Final Fantasy* creator Sakaguchi, it marked a prosperous time. He moved up the ranks as the top creative figure at Square (intermittently known as Squaresoft), becoming an executive vice president and a game industry celebrity. Looking back in interviews, he

Hironobu Sakaguchi

Producer and executive vice president, Square Japan;
Chairman and chief executive officer, Square USA
Bio on page 229

31

downplays his level of authority at the time, while others speak of him as someone who ran the show and made multimillion dollar decisions more or less on a whim.

[Note: For interviewees who worked on the PlayStation version of Final Fantasy VII, *we've listed their job titles at the time of the game's release in 1997. For those involved in other parts of this story, we've listed their titles alongside the years they held those roles.]*

Motonori Sakakibara
Movie director, Square Japan

In the late '90s, all the game companies had lots of money – especially Square, of course. So Square prioritised quality rather than obsessing over costs. That was how Sakaguchi-san operated. He always asked for a lot from the team and gave us tight schedules, but he backed up those requests with big teams and the best hardware. That was a very rare situation. He was always looking at a big vision but, at the same time, how to make it a reality.

Tomoyuki Takechi
President and chief executive officer, Square

He was always looking at the future and always had a big-picture vision. He was never satisfied with what he was currently working on.

Tatsuya Yoshinari
Programmer, Square Japan

I think calling him a god would be going too far, but it kind of felt like that. He was a superstar.

Kyoko Higo
Assistant marketing associate, Square US

I remember us calling him 'The King' ... No, not to his face.

Junichi Yanagihara
Executive vice president, Square USA

Well, he was the king, in a good way. I think that might have started as an email address where he didn't want to use his own name, so he just used 'king' and then some number combination. And that's how we started saying, 'OK, he's the king'.

Yoshihiro Maruyama
Executive vice president, Square US

Yeah, 'king,' yeah. [Laughs] Actually, you know, at most of the management meetings at Squaresoft in Japan, without him, there were no decisions made. He told the management committee when a game was going to be completed and what kind of marketing he wanted to have. So yeah, he was the king. He was controlling the entire operation.

Hironobu Sakaguchi
Producer and executive vice president, Square Japan;
Chairman and chief executive officer, Square USA

'King?' Is that from Square US? ... Those punks. [Laughs] Yeah, I remember being called that at one point. The actual meaning is very different, though. There was a time when I really drank a lot of champagne, so I got the nickname 'Champagne King'. That's where it came from. It didn't have anything to do with my work. And I don't drink like that any more.

Yoshihiro Maruyama
Executive vice president, Square US

I think the way he works is very aggressive sometimes. But he understood the creative elements and also the management issues [at Square]. He also worked very closely with key members of the development team, which no other management members of Squaresoft could do.

Hiroshi Kawai
Character programmer, Square Japan

He's very politically adept. Some of it, perhaps, could be real manipulation; some of it could be something on a more motivational side. But he knows how to get people to do things for him.

Steve Gray
Vice president of game production, Square USA

He was somebody who was very, very successful and knew what he wanted and he was just willing to have people plugging away at things until he got what he wanted. I'm not sure he always really knew, so I think there's a certain amount of randomness, you know? Stuff just getting done and then, when he liked something, he would say, 'Ah ha, that's the one'.

Tatsuya Yoshinari
Programmer, Square Japan
I wouldn't say he made arbitrary decisions, but he tended to make pretty big decisions quickly and easily. I got the feeling he made decisions based on what inspired him at the time. Something would just kind of hit him and he'd be like, 'OK, we've got to do this'.

Hironobu Sakaguchi
Producer and executive vice president, Square Japan;
chairman and chief executive officer, Square USA
I guess my style can be a little haphazard. One morning I might say to the staff, 'Do it this way'. And then, when they show me what they've done, which is what I asked for, I'll get mad: 'Why is it like this?!' That kind of thing happens from time to time. The thing is, my thoughts are always in flux, swirling around and changing in my head, so I might shoot off 10 emails in a row on the same subject. Send an email, change my mind, send another email, think about it some more.

Kyoko Higo
Assistant marketing associate, Square US
He's the father of *Final Fantasy*. He created this series. And so it was kind of easy for me and probably everyone else on our team to just kind of believe in his creation and be able to stand by it and really commit ourselves.

Yoshihiro Maruyama
Executive vice president, Square US
I think the golden days of Sakaguchi were when he was developing *FFVII*. And most of the decisions he made paid off.

2.2
Square's first attempt at making *Final Fantasy VII*

By the early '90s, Square had an unqualified hit with the *Final Fantasy* series in Japan, a growing stable of games and enough breathing room to experiment. Sakaguchi took the opportunity to dabble in a series of ambitious projects, including a high-profile collaboration with the creator of role-playing series *Dragon Quest* and the artist behind manga series *Dragon Ball*. Their result was an RPG called *Chrono Trigger*.

Meanwhile, after six *Final Fantasy* games on Nintendo hardware, Sakaguchi had begun to step away from working in the trenches on the series. Square team members Yoshinori Kitase and Tetsuya Nomura had begun to take leadership roles over day-to-day work on the *Final Fantasy* series, overseeing Sakaguchi's high-level plans and story ideas. Kitase had long been a film buff who liked the parallels between movie and game storytelling. Nomura came to the series as an artist, gradually taking on more creative responsibility.

FFVII was an obvious next step but, with console hardware advancing quickly, Square wasn't sure how to approach the game. It could play things safe and stick to the 2D pixel-art style of previous games, it could risk a new art style on aging hardware, or it could

Yoshinori Kitase

Director, Square Japan
Bio on page 228

dabble with early 3D graphics on new machines. Ideas spilled in every direction, and over the course of two years the company made three distinct attempts at getting the game off the ground.

The first of those three was a direct 2D sequel to *Final Fantasy VI* for the Super Famicom.

Yoshinori Kitase
Director, Square Japan
At the time, it wasn't clear yet whether Japanese RPGs were going to go 3D or not. Sakaguchi-san was especially fond of pixel art, and we debated a lot about whether we should remain in that 2D style ... After we finished *Final Fantasy VI*, we began working on *Final Fantasy VII* [as a 2D game for the Super Famicom], brainstorming and holding initial planning meetings.

Hironobu Sakaguchi
Producer and executive vice president, Square Japan;
chairman and chief executive officer, Square USA
1994? Ah, oh ... that ... wait, what? Kitase said that? Are you sure he's not just making it up? No, I don't know. I'm sorry, I don't remember that. Maybe he meant that he had the idea in his head.

Yoshinori Kitase
Director, Square Japan
I think we had about 60 people in total working on *FFVI*. When we started preproduction for *FFVII* [for the Super Famicom], it was probably a little smaller than that, maybe 20–30 people.

Tetsuya Nomura
Character and battle visual director, Square Japan
We were working pretty slowly on it. Maybe for a few months?

Yoshinori Kitase
Director, Square Japan
About two to three months.

Tetsuya Nomura
Character and battle visual director, Square Japan
At that early point we were all still going back and forth about what the story should be. Nothing had been clearly decided on yet … [In] the first plot treatment that Sakaguchi-san wrote, it took place in New York, there was an organisation there that was trying to destroy the Mako Reactors and a character named Detective Joe was investigating them. There were other characters involved, too. One of the members of this organisation trying to destroy the reactor was the prototype character for [eventual *FFVII* lead protagonist] Cloud.

Yoshinori Kitase
Director, Square Japan
I think I remember that you wrote some concept/planning documents too, right?

Tetsuya Nomura
Character and battle visual director, Square Japan
I did. I did.

Yoshinori Kitase
Director, Square Japan
But at that time *Chrono Trigger*'s development was in dire straits so all the team members switched over to help with *Chrono Trigger* … and that's as far as it went.

Hironobu Sakaguchi
Producer and executive vice president, Square Japan;
chairman and chief executive officer, Square USA
Ah, yes, that's right. I remember now. It was when we consolidated every-one on *Chrono Trigger*. That's right. Before we made *Chrono Trigger*, we had talked about making *FFVII* but then we moved everyone over to the *Chrono Trigger* team. I do recall now; I did write a scenario for *FFVII*, a different story [than the one we eventually used]. I don't remember it

being in New York though. You know, I think the New York idea might be from *Parasite Eve*. And Joe, that's actually the original name I had for the protagonist from *Lost Odyssey*. I don't know, maybe all this information is getting mixed up somewhere.

2.3
An early experiment in 3D graphics

Setting aside work on the Super Famicom version of *Final Fantasy VII*, Square began to explore options for where to take the series in 3D. In 1994, that was a new concept for the company and most of its staff had only been trained to make games in 2D. So rather than jump in head first, Square decided to put together a small experiment.

Using high-end machines from 3D hardware powerhouse Silicon Graphics, Inc., Square put together a tech demo showing what the characters from *Final Fantasy VI* could look like in a 3D battle scene. Team members say they always thought of the demo as a research project rather than as something they'd sell to players one day.

Behind the scenes, the process of making a 3D tech demo started with Kazuyuki Hashimoto, an engineer who had experience in early 3D game development working with companies such as Sega, Nintendo and Sony.

Hironobu Sakaguchi
Producer and executive vice president, Square Japan;
chairman and chief executive officer, Square USA
Prior to *Final Fantasy VII* ... we didn't have anyone on staff to do 3D graphics. Then I met [Hashimoto], who is my best friend to this day, and he helped me find a very talented crew to head up the visuals. It was their first time working on a game, and it was our first time working with 3D graphics.

Kazuyuki Hashimoto
CG supervisor, Square Japan; chief technical officer and
senior vice president, Square USA
At that time, I also had invites from other companies. But I wasn't interested. Sakaguchi-san was different. I think he's talented. He has something. I don't know what he has but he has something ... He has the talent or ability to see what will happen in the future.

Hironobu Sakaguchi
Producer and executive vice president, Square Japan;
chairman and chief executive officer, Square USA
We knew Nintendo 64 and PlayStation were going to be the next hard-

ware generation, and that we'd be developing our next game for one of them. It was similar to when we moved from the Famicom to the Super Famicom. Our first step wasn't to choose between the two systems, but to focus on learning the Silicon Graphics workstations we had purchased. They were very expensive machines, and we made a demo on them to show people, 'This is how *Final Fantasy* could look in 3D'.

Kazuyuki Hashimoto
CG supervisor, Square Japan; chief technical officer and senior vice president, Square USA

Square planned to build a game for the next-gen Nintendo machine, but the [development] kit wasn't available and the technical [specs kept changing]. So I suggested we could go with a standard environment and we could see what we could do with it. Then later on we could optimise this idea to the small machine. Initially, we could do something with the most powerful environment so we could be more free – free to figure out what we could do in 3D.

Hironobu Sakaguchi
Producer and executive vice president, Square Japan; chairman and chief executive officer, Square USA

Back then, it was a big step from 2D to 3D. And it was difficult even in my head to picture what the battle scenes should look like.

Kazuyuki Hashimoto
CG supervisor, Square Japan; chief technical officer and senior vice president, Square USA

Square was very new to the 3D graphics industry, so Silicon Graphics didn't pay much attention to us. After we made this demo, we wanted to show it at the SIGGRAPH conference in Los Angeles, and we couldn't bring over a machine from Japan [because it was too large]. We needed to lease a rental from the SGI headquarters, and they didn't recognise us. But I had a friend at Silicon Graphics in the US, and I asked him to coordinate a loan, so we successfully loaned one machine for the demonstration.

Hiroshi Kawai
Character programmer, Square Japan

Because I was the only developer [on the team who spoke English], I was tasked with manning the booth and explaining how the game worked at SIGGRAPH. While the demo had only one battle, I remember it being fun to play ... I remember most people wanting a second or third go to figure out the right pattern of commands to win the game.

Hironobu Sakaguchi
Producer and executive vice president, Square Japan;
chairman and chief executive officer, Square USA
There wasn't that big of a crowd. We made it so people could draw a symbol on the screen to cast a spell or call out a dragon. And they were interested in the visuals, but the mechanics seemed to confuse them.

Michael Jones
Engineering director, Silicon Graphics (1992–1999)
Their user interface was a gestural interface. So you'd make the Zorro 'Z' and that meant something. And you'd make a circle and that meant something. These were gestures as understood by storytelling game people, not gestures as understood by Microsoft working on an operating system UI or something. It was much more aggressive and imaginative, and maybe a little less reasonable, but more fun. You know, if a computer company had made a pinball machine, they would have had a button that says 'push' or 'launch' or 'click' or something, but if you had a game designer, it would have a big spring and a thing you pull back on.

Kazuyuki Hashimoto
CG supervisor, Square Japan; chief technical officer and
senior vice president, Square USA
People at the show didn't understand what they were looking at. A lot of them were interested in high-tech engineering or military-related things for business purposes, and we demonstrated this game just for fun. People said, 'Oh, interesting.' That's it. But I still remember Michael Jones at SGI came to visit because we used this technology, and he was so impressed that he said SGI really wanted to demonstrate the application in its headquarters in Mountain View [California]. And we gave him the executable to demonstrate the game at the SGI headquarters. He went on to became the head of Keyhole. Do you know what that is? It's Google Earth. Anyway, small world.

Michael Jones
Engineering director, Silicon Graphics (1992–1999)
What I liked about it, just personally, was that, even though they were advanced technically, they were actually faithful – unlike other videogames – they were faithful to anime. You know, in *Akira*, the guy raises his fist up in the air and something happens, right? In videogames of the day, [they sort of had] a poor take on that. So this game was, 'Let's make a computer game that looks like the artform that inspired this game.'

Hironobu Sakaguchi
Producer and executive vice president, Square Japan;
chairman and chief executive officer, Square USA

At the time, when you were talking about computer graphics, people wanted to see something very realistic, something that you could throw into a live action movie and they couldn't tell the difference. But we used CG to represent anime characters. Because of that, I think a lot of people at the show weren't very interested in it. But that's what we wanted to do.

Michael Jones
Engineering director, Silicon Graphics (1992–1999)

We had a lot of customers who did crazy things. Customers that simulated nuclear reactors. Customers that taught astronauts to fly a space shuttle. All these kinds of lunatic fringe applications, they liked using our computers, and often they liked using my team's software. And, in particular, machines like that, even if they're kind of over the top as far as what a gamer would use, they're great for game designers and developers because they can simulate interactively what would later on take maybe a year to code up to be interactive on a PC or something ... You know, you can practise basically by using a computer of super power ... And so that's what Square had done, pretty much.

2.4
Square's second attempt at making *Final Fantasy VII*

With *Chrono Trigger* behind it and work on the *Final Fantasy* SIGGRAPH tech demo underway, Square began to take steps toward a second attempt at making *FFVII*, following the abandoned Super Famicom project. Square had long been a Nintendo ally, making most of its games exclusively for Nintendo's systems, so many at the company assumed they would follow whatever Nintendo did next and make games for the company's new console, the Nintendo 64.

Nintendo even had a partnership with Silicon Graphics for its

Nintendo 64 hardware, making what some thought would be a natural transition using the company's experience from the SIGGRAPH demo.

While working on a variety of other projects, Square began to put together a plan for what a 3D *FFVII* could look like on the Nintendo 64. The concept involved making the game for Nintendo's 64DD peripheral, a disc drive add-on that ended up only shipping in Japan and never taking off commercially. Square team members say they wanted to include lengthy cutscenes and large amounts of content in the game, which would have been difficult in the limited space of a Nintendo 64 cartridge, but

that plan never got far enough into development to have anything substantial to show publicly.

Yoshinori Kitase
Director, Square Japan
It wasn't really officially in development for the Nintendo 64. It was more like we were experimenting with the hardware.

Hiroshi Kawai
Character programmer, Square Japan
[Nintendo] actually started giving us emulation kits for the 64. They weren't running on anything reasonably sized. Do you know what an SGI Onyx looks like? A little smaller than [a 4'×4'] table ... I only had very simple demos running on it at the time, trying to port over some of the higher-resolution models that we used for the SIGGRAPH demo to see how they would perform ... I was [also] using a 3D model of a Leviathan guardian that definitely wasn't part of the *FFVI* SIGGRAPH demo.

Yoshinori Kitase
Director, Square Japan
We started making a demo to see what was possible, and only a handful of people worked on it: a few programmers, and four or five artists to work on the graphics. Those artists may have forgotten by now, but the first characters we had them work on were Cloud, Barret and Red XIII [all of whom ended up in the final version of *Final Fantasy VII*].

Tetsuya Nomura
Character and battle visual director, Square Japan
I remember working on them and revising their initial designs. Cloud and Barret were too short, so I made them taller. Yeah, the three of them were probably the first characters we made.

Yoshinori Kitase
Director, Square Japan
A small group of us worked on those ideas in secret and gradually added more people.

52

Tetsuya Nomura
Character and battle visual director, Square Japan
It all took place in one room too, I remember.

Yoshinori Kitase
Director, Square Japan
Yeah. It was a single room segregated from everyone else. Very few people knew about and worked on the project. It was all hush-hush. As for the main bulk of the work on that demo, maybe it took a month or two?

Tetsuya Nomura
Character and battle visual director, Square Japan
It's hard to say what the exact time frame was. There wasn't a schedule, really.

Yoshinori Kitase
Director, Square Japan
Nomura, do you remember, when we were making that SGI demo for the Nintendo 64, that the first thing you created was the Behemoth model?

Tetsuya Nomura
Character and battle visual director, Square Japan
I did? In polygons?

Yoshinori Kitase
Director, Square Japan
Whenever we're doing research and development on a new *Final Fantasy* game, we usually select Behemoth as a test model of sorts. For the Nintendo 64 demo, it took 2,000 polygons to render him.

Tetsuya Nomura
Character and battle visual director, Square Japan
I don't remember that at all.

Yoshinori Kitase
Director, Square Japan
You don't? But you designed him! [Laughs] Anyway, we made a 2,000-count polygon version of Behemoth for the Nintendo 64, but when we rendered and animated it, the framerate was way too low. To properly display Behemoth with that technology, we needed 2,000 polygons, but it was a little too much for the hardware. That was part of the problem with choosing Nintendo.

Hiroshi Kawai
Character programmer, Square Japan

All this work was toward – I think they called it the Shoshinkai, Nintendo's Space World [trade show in Japan]. And here I am coding, kind of being able to do lead dev work for this Space World demo. Then I think it was near the end of the year. Sakaguchi-san just gathers everybody in the middle of this gigantic floor where we had a bunch of devs working in the middle of Meguro. And he just casually announces, 'You know, we're not developing for Nintendo anymore' ... So all my work at that point kind of went down the drain.

Tetsuya Nomura

'I remember walking down the hall when Sakaguchi-san stopped me and said, 'Hey, look
at this!' He was wearing this jumper jacket, and
he turned around and showed me the Play-
Station logo on the back. I stood there kind
of dumbfounded.'

2.5
Square leaves Nintendo, aligns with Sony

In the Super Famicom era, Nintendo had a chokehold on many of the big Japanese third-party game studios. Companies such as Capcom, Konami and Square played key roles in Nintendo's success, and prioritised Nintendo's hardware over Sega's Mega Drive/Genesis.

As the Nintendo 64 and Play-Station arrived, that grip began to loosen. Despite Sony having an unproven track record in the game industry, its developer outreach and hardware convinced many third-party teams to hop on board. Square was one of the biggest studios to jump ship, announcing in early 1996 that it had decided to shift its entire lineup to Sony's hardware, with *Final Fantasy VII* as the centrepiece.

By the end of the generation, almost all major third-party studios had signed up with Sony, in part due to the economic advantages of manufacturing games on PlayStation's CDs compared to Nintendo 64's cartridges.

Yoshihiro Maruyama
Executive vice president, Square US
[In September 1995] I was hired by the president of the company, [Tetsuo] Mizuno-san, and he told me that, 'Squaresoft will always be with Nintendo ... As long as you work for us, it's basically the same as working for Nintendo.' And the week after I joined, they started saying, 'Oh, maybe we should switch to Sony.' So I was kind of shocked.

Tetsuya Nomura
Character and battle visual director, Square Japan
I remember walking down the hall when Sakaguchi-san stopped me and said, 'Hey, look at this!' He was wearing this jumper jacket, and he turned around and showed me the PlayStation logo on the back. I stood there

kind of dumbfounded ... I was pretty low on the totem pole at Square back then, so I couldn't really say anything in response – and, in any event, even if he had talked to me about it, I was only in a position to nod and agree with him.

Yoshinori Kitase
Director, Square Japan
I think [we announced the move to Sony with] a TV commercial, right?

Tetsuya Nomura
Character and battle visual director, Square Japan
Ah, yeah. I think so. It was kind of unusual to use a TV commercial to announce that a game was under development ... We don't do that kind of announcement nowadays.

Yoshinori Kitase
Director, Square Japan
I also remember that we put an ad out in *Shonen Jump* [magazine], which had a circulation of six million people. We put that out at the same time we released the TV ad, and I think together they had a huge impact.

Keith Boesky
President, Eidos (1997–1999)
Square was a bet-the-company kind of company. It was a big risk to put *Final Fantasy VII* on the PlayStation ... Nobody had confidence in PlayStation. Nobody knew whether it would work, and most people thought that it wouldn't. And the early pictures that came out, when it looked like a toilet bowl, confirmed everybody's suspicions.

Yoshitaka Amano
Image illustrator, freelance
That must have been a huge decision for [Sakaguchi] to make. But he did it, and from there the series grew dramatically. It's amazing that he was able to do that and make it work. He did that all for the game, his series.

Yoshinori Kitase
Director, Square Japan
I think it was a very difficult time for our president and for Sakaguchi-san.

Hironobu Sakaguchi
*Producer and executive vice president, Square Japan;
chairman and chief executive officer, Square USA*

Of course, back then I wasn't the president of Square. There was a management level above me, and I talked with them to make the decision. But PlayStation games being on CDs was the biggest factor. If you wanted to make a 3D action game on a Nintendo 64 cartridge with its limited space, you could do it. But I wanted to create a 3D role-playing game. It was very clear in my head what I wanted to make, but that would have been difficult on Nintendo's hardware ...

The biggest problem was, of course, memory. Based on our calculations there was no way it could all fit on a ROM cartridge. So our main reason for choosing the PlayStation was really just because it was the only console which would allow us to use CD-ROM media.

Tomoyuki Takechi
President and chief executive officer, Square
Also CDs were cheaper than cartridges, so we were thinking we could provide more to players without raising the price. That was another big part of the appeal.

Hironobu Sakaguchi
Producer and executive vice president, Square Japan;
Chairman and chief executive officer, Square USA
The costs were just completely different. On average, a cartridge cost players around ¥10,000, and CDs were about half of that. Nintendo was fully confident that they could still be a hit and push forward at that price and sell tons of games. We weren't entirely in agreement with that because we looked at other forms of entertainment like music and movies and they were much cheaper ... For people to pay ¥10,000 versus being able to enjoy, you know, a brand new music album for $20, we just couldn't get over that. We didn't agree with that model. And on top of that, the method of distribution was very different. Nintendo was basically operating in a toy category whereas Sony came from a music and film background. And we didn't necessarily feel that going the toy category route was going to be a better answer for us.

[Note: While many people speaking for this story point to this often-told story about the differences between CD-ROMs and cartridges as the main reason for Square's shift to PlayStation, some say hardware horsepower differences and communication between Square and Nintendo also played a key role in the decision. Kawai says he believes Square has focused its public comments on the disc versus cartridge debate over the years out of respect to Nintendo.]

Shinichiro Kajitani
Vice president, Square USA

Around that time, Sony approached us, and told us, 'We have the Play-Station coming out and we want to make 3D games. Would you guys be interested?' And at the time, since we were really close to Nintendo, we said, 'Well, we're not sure. We're pretty much just working with them'. And I asked if it was OK to share that information with Nintendo. And Sony said, 'That's totally fine. Go ahead and show it to them. We just want you to see what we're doing, and if you like it, then by all means, come work with us on this.' It's not that we were passing information back and forth between Nintendo and Sony, but at the time our programmers ... started making prototypes that ran on the PlayStation and Nintendo 64 as sort of benchmark software to test each system.

Tatsuya Yoshinari
Programmer, Square Japan

We were trying to work out whether to do it with the Nintendo machine or not ... There was a while there where we were going back and forth between the N64 and PlayStation, seeing what we could do with 3D graphics on each system.

Motonori Sakakibara
Movie director, Square Japan

I saw a couple of the tests, but it was obviously different. The quality was so different. So I thought they'd never take Nintendo because the result was very clear.

Hiroshi Kawai
Character programmer, Square Japan

I kind of had a suspicion that things weren't going too well for the 64 at that point, because ... one of my responsibilities ... was to write performance applications that compared how well the 64 fared against the prototype [PlayStation]. And we'd be running parallel comparisons between the [PlayStation] where you'd have a bunch of 2D sprites bouncing off the screen and see how many polygons you could get within a 60th of a second. And even without any kind of texturing or any kind of lighting, it was less than 50% of what you would be able to get out of the [PlayStation]. Of course, the drawback of the [PlayStation] is it didn't really have a z-buffer, so you'd have these overlapping polygons that you'd have to work around so that you wouldn't get the shimmering [look]. But on the other hand, there was no way you'd be able to get anything close to what *FFVII* was doing [on PlayStation] on the 64 at that time.

There was actually this one trip that [Nintendo] organised for me, [main programmer Ken] Narita-san, a few other lead devs who were working on the battle portion for the *Final Fantasy VI* [SIGGRAPH] demo at that point ... I think Nintendo had been getting signals from Square saying, you know, 'Your hardware isn't up to snuff. Not only in terms of raw 3D performance, but in terms of storage'. And they said, 'We're gonna fabricate this brand new chip,' which was supposed to have a bunch of hardware improvements to get a little bit more performance. Which, my suspicion is they probably just repeated that verbatim from SGI, and I think there was, in general, a disconnect between SGI and Nintendo in terms of what they were expecting the hardware to do. SGI was probably talking more along theoretical lines of what the hardware would be able to do, and they were trying to make it general purpose so that it wasn't just a 3D rendering machine. But Nintendo had certain specific performance metrics that had to be met, but I don't think those were communicated well to SGI.

The wires just – they weren't in sync there. So they sent us down to Mountain View, and I took all that code I was writing for the Shoshinkai to run on the [latest prototype] hardware there. And it didn't really change in terms of performance.

Darren Smith
Project manager/manager, Nintendo of America (1993–2000)
In 1993, [Nintendo] asked me to take on the role leading at least the North American side of project management for the development of the next-generation console [which became the Nintendo 64], and I found that the partner was Silicon Graphics. So I moved down to California and was the person from Nintendo on-site there full time, coordinating the work between Japan and what was going on on-site there at SGI ...

We definitely met with [Square]. We met with almost every single publisher out there, really just to give them background on the technology, what it was capable of. Met with [Square] a couple of times. They came back with a demo of kind of what they found the technology was capable of doing, asked questions about how to optimise things ... I have a vague recollection of what they showed. From what I recall, the demo showed an increasing number of 2D bouncing balls with some textures mapped onto them. I don't think they showed anything that showed gameplay, or even anything with their own [intellectual property] attached to it.

Hiroshi Kawai
Character programmer, Square Japan
We spent a few days, I remember, optimising my code, to try to get a

few more polygons out, but it didn't really make much of a difference. And upon returning to Tokyo, there was a meeting with me, Narita-san, Sakaguchi-san and the major stakeholder of Square, Miyamoto-san. And I had never seen [Miyamoto in person before then]. He just comes in. 'OK so, how was it?' And I gave a few figures when asked, but Narita-san was the main person who was talking. And he was essentially saying, 'We're just not getting the performance. We're nowhere near what we did during the SIGGRAPH demo.' Miyamoto-san just silently acknowledged that, and I didn't hear anything from them until the point when Sakaguchi-san called [the office] together and said, 'We're not doing the 64 anymore.' So yeah. I guess in a sense, I kind of provided the objective data to say that the 64 wasn't suitable for the next-gen *Final Fantasy*.

Shinichiro Kajitani
Vice president, Square USA
At that time, Square was really close to Nintendo – we were basically like a second party for them. So when their new system was in development, we gave them lots of advice, like, 'You're going to need a CD-ROM drive for it,' 'You don't have enough bandwidth to do what we're trying to do,' and, 'With what you have now, we're not going to be able to make an RPG.' We gave them lots of advice. But [Nintendo president Hiroshi] Yamauchi-san at Nintendo basically refused to listen to any of it. And that's when Sakaguchi-san and the management team at Square decided, 'OK, we're going to go with Sony now.'

Hironobu Sakaguchi
Producer and executive vice president, Square Japan;
chairman and chief executive officer, Square USA
We made our pitch as a team to the president and founder of Square, Miyamoto-san, because ultimately it was going to come down to whether it made business sense. Miyamoto-san encouraged us: if we, the software designers, were confident that we could make a good game this way, then it would be strange to deny us this opportunity. He agreed that this was the way to go and told us to do as we saw fit.

Junichi Yanagihara
Executive vice president, Square USA
[Miyamoto-san] has this sort of business sense, a spontaneous reaction to something new ... Some people may take their time to think something through, whether it is a good idea for the company or not. I got the impression that Miyamoto-san is someone who just says, 'Oh OK I think this is a great idea. We'll do it.' Rather than doing due diligence and so forth.

Tomoyuki Takechi
President and chief executive officer, Square
Sony basically gave us the best deal they were giving to any publisher. And they did a lot of public relations work and marketing on their dime. They gave us a great deal to help convince us to come over ... I can't talk about the details, but one thing I can say is that Sony went very low on the per-unit royalties that we had to pay.

Shigeo Maruyama
Chairman, Sony Computer Entertainment
It was obvious to them how much we wanted the deal. We didn't even have to lure them with the promotional campaigns we were going to run because they could tell from our enthusiasm that we were going all-in. It was the pure energy that Sony was pouring into the deal.

Shuhei Yoshida
Square account manager, Sony Computer Entertainment
I was actually one of the publisher relations [team members], an account manager of Square, so I know more than I can talk about ... It's a long story getting into that announcement.

Shigeo Maruyama
Chairman, Sony Computer Entertainment
We had a guy named Yuji Takahashi negotiate the deal with Square. Takechi-san told Takahashi that unless PlayStation sold more than three million units in Japan, they couldn't develop *FFVII* for it. That was because of the manufacturing cost. They knew ahead of time that they would be in the red if they manufactured and sold a million copies. Three million was probably their break-even point. So Square told us that it was our job to sell three million units, and then they would consider developing for PlayStation. It was a daunting number, for sure. But, for them as a business, it made complete sense. You don't want to venture into something that isn't going to be profitable.

Hironobu Sakaguchi
Producer and executive vice president, Square Japan;
chairman and chief executive officer, Square USA
I wasn't directly involved with the negotiations ... But with any negotiation, you're going to have to bluff a little bit, so it wouldn't surprise me if we didn't need Sony to sell quite that many.

Tomoyuki Takechi

President and chief executive officer, Square
Bio on page 229

Shigeo Maruyama
Chairman, Sony Computer Entertainment

We knew that Square's developers wanted to work on PlayStation, so the pressure was on the CEO because, as the head of the company, he couldn't make risky decisions lightly. As soon as we hit three million units sold, Takahashi-san approached him again saying, 'We did our part. Now you can do yours.'

Yoshitaka Amano
Image illustrator, freelance

To be honest, [I don't remember the shift to 3D being a big deal]. The thing I remember more was that *Final Fantasy* was no longer going to be a Famicom game; it was going to be a PlayStation game. That fact had more of an impact.

Shigeo Maruyama
Chairman, Sony Computer Entertainment

By that point, most of the heavy hitters had already come to PlayStation. The only remaining ones were *Final Fantasy* and *Dragon Quest*. We were confident that once *Final Fantasy* made the jump, the majority of the remaining third-party titles would follow. So, that was a big deal.

Shuhei Yoshida
Square account manager, Sony Computer Entertainment

It was amazing. Everything changed after ... *FFVII* and *Dragon Quest VII* [from Square rival publisher Enix] was like a one-two [punch] ... At least for the Japanese market, that really made the PlayStation the most popular console for the generation.

Hironobu Sakaguchi
Producer and executive vice president, Square Japan;
chairman and chief executive officer, Square USA

Politically, it was a drastic change and a huge decision, but for me it was more of a natural decision because that was the hardware we needed to make the game.

Jun Iwasaki
Vice president of marketing, Square US

I thought it was the right decision, but yeah, there was a lot of [tension] with Nintendo after.

Tomoyuki Takechi
President and chief executive officer, Square
It was pretty uncomfortable. There were about four to five years where we couldn't really talk with Nintendo. We didn't have a friendly relationship with them.

Shinichiro Kajitani
Vice president, Square USA
When we made the decision to go with Sony, for about 10 years we basically weren't allowed into Nintendo's offices. From a consumer's point of view, it was good to have two companies competing with each other because prices wouldn't rise and it would be better for them. But from a business perspective, our main interest was making sure that Sony won and Nintendo lost, basically, because that would be better for us.

George Harrison
Senior vice president, marketing and communications,
Nintendo of America (1992–2007)
The period when PlayStation first arrived using CDs rather than cartridges was a tough period for Nintendo with publishers. Nintendo wanted to stay with cartridges to minimise counterfeiting but publishers wanted the extra capacity available on CDs. This was especially true for games like *Final Fantasy* with rich graphics.

Darren Smith
Project manager/manager, Nintendo of America (1993–2000)
I knew it was important [when Square left], and it certainly was a loss. But for me, it wasn't such a devastating loss. I knew it was important for [Nintendo in] Japan. I'm not so sure about the US market. We knew it was a big deal to have lost it on our system and, knowing that it would make Sony a bigger competitor, it made the work that much more important.

Hiroshi Kawai
Character programmer, Square Japan
I'll say this. I'm impressed with what Nintendo [was] able to do with the 64 hardware. *Mario, Zelda* – their devs must be top notch to be able to do that. But that's essentially the extent of what you can do with the hardware. And you would get nowhere near anything like a *Final Fantasy* running on it.

Hironobu Sakaguchi
Producer and executive vice president, Square Japan;
chairman and chief executive officer, Square USA

When we made our decision, the president of Square [Masafumi Miyamoto], our lead programmer [Ken Narita] and I went to a meeting with Yamauchi-san. There is an old cultural tradition where, in Kyoto, someone will welcome you with tea, but you're not supposed to really drink that tea. It's just polite to have it there. And Yamauchi-san welcomed us with a very expensive bento meal and beer, and gave us a very nice welcome and basically patted us on the back to say, 'I wish you the best.' No bitter feelings or anything.

Hiroshi Kawai
Character programmer, Square Japan
I think [Sakaguchi] is just trying to be politically correct with that one.

Yoshihiro Maruyama
Executive vice president, Square US
I don't think [anyone from Nintendo gave us a hard time]. They said, 'Oh, we don't need that.' That's what they said. [Laughs] Their philosophy has always been that Nintendo hardware is for their games, and if a publisher wants to publish, 'OK you can do it.' But if you don't like it, 'We don't want you.'

Hiroshi Kawai
Character programmer, Square Japan
What I heard was Nintendo said, 'If you're leaving us, never come back.'

[Note: In October 2001, then Square president Hisashi Suzuki said in an interview with the Nihon Keizai Shimbun that Nintendo became especially frustrated not when Square left, but because of public statements Square made criticising Nintendo management, and because Square helped convince Enix to leave as well. Suzuki declined an interview request for this book.]

Hironobu Sakaguchi
Producer and executive vice president, Square Japan;
chairman and chief executive officer, Square USA
I don't actually know any part of that story [with Enix] … I wonder if people now feel like there was more tension than there really was because the game ended up being such a hit … Maybe it looks like it was more tense in retrospect because this was the first game in the series with Sony, and that makes it convenient to suggest that Nintendo missed out on this big success. I think that might have something to do with it.

Game

3

3.1
Square spends big on *Final Fantasy VII*'s development

After settling on its decision to leave Nintendo, Square moved quickly to make *FFVII* a reality on PlayStation, hiring a large 3D tech and art staff and purchasing hundreds of Silicon Graphics workstations. For many team members, that financial backing made all the difference, enabling them to outpace many of their competitors working in early 3D game development.

Meanwhile, Square put its top resources into the game's art, music and plot, experimenting with the best ways to tell a story with polygonal characters and

CG cutscenes. It also spent money opening a new Western sales and marketing office in the US to help promote the game in territories where the series hadn't yet taken off.

From front to back, Square spared little expense in its attempts to make and promote the game.

Yoshihiro Maruyama
Executive vice president, Square US
Final Fantasy VII came very quickly; the development period was a little more than a year. That was very unusual at the time ... To shorten the development cycle, they invested hugely into the technology. The team expanded to close to 150 all of a sudden, from like 30–40 people.

Keith Boesky
President, Eidos (1997–1999)
They had 150 people working on the game, which was a huge number. A normal game team was 20 at the time.

[Note: Some remember the staffing numbers differently than Maruyama and Boesky. In an interview for this book, director Yoshinori Kitase estimates that Final Fantasy VI*'s development team comprised 60 people. And a 1997 issue of Japanese magazine* Weekly Famitsu *reports that Square used 200 people to develop* FFVII. *FFVI's credits list 65 names, with 16 of those appearing in the Special Thanks section.* FFVII*'s credits list more than 350 names, with over 200 of those from outsourcing partners and overseas offices.]*

Junichi Yanagihara
Executive vice president, Square USA
Myself, Hashimoto-san and Kajitani-san were sort of three pals. We basi-
cally had to go around the world recruiting people.

Shinichiro Kajitani
Vice president, Square USA
I was involved in recruiting, yeah ... It wasn't really that difficult, because
starting around '92 or '93 we decided that, because of the way the industry was going, we should start focusing more on 3D graphics. And
at the time, there were magazines called *Nikkei CG* and *Pixel*, and we
found about 100 or so names through those. So we went around talking
to them. For one of those trips we actually went to Skywalker Ranch. I
didn't meet George Lucas myself, but I saw him off in the distance. At the
time, there were only about 10 Japanese people working there in the film
studio, but I went and talked to all of them.

Hiroshi Kawai
Character programmer, Square Japan
Do you know a company called Recruit in Japan? They're pretty big.
They publish a lot of magazines, but one of the most important mag-
azines they publish is sort of like a help-wanted magazine. [Like clas-
sified ads] but more extravagant. They do in-depth interviews with
people in the company to [showcase what it's like to work there].
Companies would sort of vie to get themselves listed in this magazine.
[Square sent me a copy] out of the blue, and I think the reason was that I
was one of the few Japanese speakers at MIT.

Shinichiro Kajitani
Vice president, Square USA
Square was always of the mind that it would be best to commit 100 percent to just one thing, so where, for example, Sega would buy a $10,000
machine, Square would buy a $100,000 machine. Then when we'd go out
to recruit designers and programmers, they would say, 'Well, we'd rather
work with the $100,000 machine.'

Hiroshi Kawai
Character programmer, Square Japan
It was a very developer-friendly environment ... We were only able to do
what we were doing because the company was financially healthy.

76

Yoshitaka Amano
Image illustrator, freelance

I felt the budget getting bigger and the scale getting bigger. It didn't feel like a domestic thing any more; it felt like something that was going worldwide and becoming more global and more important. But I didn't really get paid more.

Steve Gray
Vice president of game production, Square USA

This was when Square really had a lot of money and you had these unlimited, no rules expense accounts, which is a nice thing to have in Tokyo ... I mean, when I started the *Parasite Eve* project, I tried to make a schedule and a budget. [Sakaguchi] kind of looked at it and was like, 'Whatever. Why are you doing this?'

Hiroshi Kawai
Character programmer, Square Japan

There was a great push to get our dev environment up to speed so that we could effectively develop at full speed. All the game designers had an SGI on their desk. They had a PC on their desk. [Square] spent a lot of money on infrastructure. And I know Hashimoto-san probably had a large purse to work with, just to try to get the best 3D artists.

Kazuyuki Hashimoto
CG supervisor, Square Japan; chief technical officer and senior vice president, Square USA

At that time, every workstation cost $70,000. At first, when we were working on the SIGGRAPH demo, we ordered four machines. We were a small customer. After we moved on to *FFVII*, we asked them for a quote for 200 machines. They were surprised. 'What?!'

Tomoyuki Takechi
President and chief executive officer, Square

We used about $40 million [approximately $62 million in 2018, taking into account inflation] for the game's development. We probably spent $10 million of that just on the computer graphics.

Shinichiro Kajitani
Vice president, Square USA

At that time, I was the head of system administration, so I arranged and bought all of the equipment. [Over the course of two years] I signed cheques to Silicon Graphics totalling about $38 million. I bought more than 200 Indigo2 desktop machines, Onyx and Challenge rendering servers and other machines ...

During *FFVII*'s development, we purchased 200 to 250 Indigo2s at $70,000 apiece. An Onyx server cost about $1 million. A Challenge server cost about $500,000. So we paid a total of around $17 million on SGI equipment ... And also for software, we paid Alias approximately ¥2,000,000 multiplied by 250 for a total of around $4 million. So, excluding labour costs, we spent around $21 million on graphics hardware and software. About 90 percent of that was for *FFVII*, but we may have used it on other projects as well.

One thing that surprises me even now is that, at the time, the PlayStation development kits were about $20,000 each, and they were just sitting there in cardboard boxes in the hallway where pretty much anybody could enter off the street and grab them. And there were SGI machines sitting there too, and literally anyone could have just walked in from outside and taken one. There was pretty much no security.

3.2
Square moves quickly to make the game

In early 1996, the *Final Fantasy VII* team had much of the equipment and workforce it needed, and just under a year to finish the game. With a short development cycle, Square ensured its visuals would be at the cutting edge of early 3D games. It also meant the staff had to move quickly.

From setting up a tools pipeline to learning the hardware to ground-level programming, the team learned as it went.

Hiroki Chiba
Event planner, Square Japan
Because it was the first 3D game in the series, everything was new and everything was a challenge.

Tatsuya Yoshinari
Programmer, Square Japan

It was kind of a jolting experience to go from 2D to 3D. When I was back in school, I didn't really put much effort into technical studies and that sort of thing, and I just kind of thought about making games one way ... And then once I made the jump to 3D graphics, I realised I didn't know nearly as much math as I should. And I was really upset at myself for not studying more math in school ... I think a lot of programmers at the time were probably in the same position.

Kazuyuki Hashimoto
CG supervisor, Square Japan; chief technical officer and senior vice president, Square USA

Most of the difficulty was the in-game stuff and the tiny memory space. The SIGGRAPH tech demo used a very high-end SGI super workstation. It had 256 megabytes of memory and also 256 megabytes of texture memory. In '96, it was a big machine. Do you know how much memory was available on the PlayStation 1? Two megabytes. Only two megabytes available for the system memory and also 500K for the texture memory. It was so tiny. And the problem was the motion data. The animation data was just so huge, and we needed to think about how to shrink it.

Hiroshi Kawai
Character programmer, Square Japan

We had to be efficient in figuring out what character 3D animation data you wanted in a particular level, so that you wouldn't be spending too much time loading stuff. I remember being given this assignment where the metric that I had to meet was that all the *Final Fantasy VII* characters for the field maps – the main characters, the party characters – had to be able to be animating at 60 frames per second lined up side by side on a screen ... I did manage to achieve that with some of the optimisations that Sony reluctantly made available to us. Their original dev tools were designed in a way where ... they were hoping to make it so they could have devs work with the support of a [PlayStation] API so that wouldn't break as they made improvements under the hood. But it got to a point where [we really needed to get more out of the hardware]. And one of our devs actually disassembled their code and figured out what the hardware code instructions were to do certain calculations optimally ...

At first, Sony wasn't too keen on us accessing the hardware directly because it would require any future hardware changes to maintain the functionality we were dependent on. Fortunately, they eventually

Hiroshi Kawai

Character programmer, Square Japan
Bio on page 228

relented and, in turn, cleaned up our internal API so that it could be made available to all PlayStation developers.

Kazuyuki Hashimoto
CG supervisor, Square Japan; chief technical officer and senior vice president, Square USA
I remember seeing the lead programmer, Narita-san, struggling to make the characters walk on a 3D surface. When he solved the problem, everybody was so happy with it ... [That was an] unforgettable event.

Hiroshi Kawai
Character programmer, Square Japan
The biggest moment that I remember was – and it may have been a first for *FFVII* – where they were syncing realtime 3D with FMVs. Do you remember the opening scene where you were zooming in to the train, and then you had Cloud jumping off the train, and you had, I think, two guards standing on the train platform, who would be coming into view, being rendered in real time? I remember everything was supposed to work in theory, with all the math that we had done at that point. But as you may have heard, PlayStation – in order to get its performance – didn't have the precision of your high-end SGI machines. So you had to sort of fudge certain numerical values to approximate what it was doing on the SGI. And that moment in the initial scene where the camera just zoomed in – it wasn't a full-blown FMV at that point; it was a really simply rendered 3D background – but just to see the 3D characters and the FMV in sync was really awesome at that point.

Frank Hom
Associate producer, Eidos (1995–2001)
[The game] was just so beautiful. It was just so ahead of its time ... There just was nothing like that kind of melding of 2D and 3D art, and having the art transition from in-game to CGI back into in-game. To me, that was just awesome. It didn't take you out of the experience when you were playing the game. I think that was the beauty of *FFVII* ... You're always immersed.

Motonori Sakakibara
Movie director, Square Japan
Every day, we'd see some progression and be amazed by the result. The project lasted just one year, but the energy level was very high. I'd never seen that kind of team before.

Tatsuya Yoshinari
Programmer, Square Japan

One of the biggest factors was that everyone was highly motivated. There were a lot of people who were working on the game 24 hours a day, and no one got burned out because we were all motivated and having a good time. So while Square put a lot of money into technology and manpower, motivation was definitely also a big factor. We were young and could work long periods of time straight through ...

I spent most of my waking hours thinking about the game. I would get up in the morning and immediately start thinking about the game, go straight to work, work on the game until late at night with everyone else at Square, and then at night I'd get on the train and go home thinking about the game, get in the bathtub thinking about the game, go to sleep, and do the same thing the next day. I didn't feel like I had to work to get things done. I wanted to do it.

Kazuyuki Hashimoto

'I remember seeing the lead programmer, Narita-san, struggling to make the characters walk
on a 3D surface. When he solved the problem,
everybody was so happy with it ... [That was an]
unforgettable event.'

3.3
Artist Tetsuya Nomura moves up the ranks

While Square sorted its tech under the hood, it also needed to decide what art style *Final Fantasy VII*, as the company's first major 3D project, should have.

The game's overall appearance fell to art director Yusuke Naora. But it was character designer Tetsuya Nomura who became a star amongst fans, thanks to his characters like Cloud, whose spiky hair translated well to the screen via the game's 3D engine. Across the board, *FFVII*'s characters moved away from the super-deformed look established in the 2D *Final Fantasy* games, which

Tetsuya Nomura

Character and battle visual director, Square Japan
Bio on page 229

many say made them more palatable for Western fans at the time.

Over the course of the game's development, Nomura not only drew the cast but took some ownership of the creative side of the project as a whole, contributing to the game's story and design alongside Sakaguchi and Kitase.

In the years following *FFVII*'s release, Nomura would go on to spearhead the *Kingdom Hearts* franchise and become one of Square's highest profile employees.

Nobuo Uematsu
Music composer, Square Japan
Nomura-san had been working on the series for a long time [before *Final Fantasy VII*], but I feel like his art really came to life in the PlayStation era because you could show more on the screen. I think it worked out really well for him that the *Final Fantasy* series moved onto PlayStation.

Motonori Sakakibara
Movie director, Square Japan
Nomura-san was a great 2D artist, but his characters worked especially well in 3D. He spent a ton of time making the game characters look like

his original designs, which was one of the big secrets behind the creation of the *FFVII* characters.

Tetsuya Nomura
Character and battle visual director, Square Japan
I'd been involved with the series since *Final Fantasy V*. And on *FFV* and *VI*, I would always talk about plans and mention ideas to Kitase-san. But on *VII*, that was when I took a bit more of a leadership role and started coming up with proposals and speaking more clearly about what I wanted to do in the game.

Motonori Sakakibara
Movie director, Square Japan
Nomura-san is crazy. [Laughs] His standards were extremely high. He was always concerned about the characters' eyes, for example – the shapes and sizes of the eyes, the thicknesses of the eyelids. He'd spend a ton of time just on a little curve of an eye. I don't think he ever gave me a simple approval.

Tetsuya Nomura
Character and battle visual director, Square Japan
I'm a little bit fickle, so I'm not the type of person to work on one thing and focus simply on that. Say, if I'm drawing – I wouldn't work on one single piece at a time. It would be more like four or five and I'd rotate between them. Or if I'm working on a design document for a game and I feel I need a change of pace, I'll start drawing something instead. Or, if I need to draw, I might work on different projects to change my mood and get that sort of refresh. So that's how I prioritise those kinds of things. But if there is a deadline, of course I'll prioritise that first.

Hiroshi Kawai
Character programmer, Square Japan
I might sound a little condescending here, but he seemed like a very dedicated artist back during *FFVII*. I don't know what about *VII* itself, or perhaps it was actually *Final Fantasy VIII*, that changed the tide, but he seemed to become a very different person at that point, where the authority that he gained from *FFVII* and *FFVIII* got to a point where he became sort of untouchable in a similar vein as Sakaguchi-san. You couldn't really fight against him.

Tetsuya Nomura
Character and battle visual director, Square Japan

93

Between when I started at Square and now, my position within the company has changed a lot. So when I started, I was kind of at the bottom rung of the corporate chain, and now I'm at a level where I'm making executive decisions. So, on that level, it's changed, but my stance has always been to look at things from the player's perspective. Some people might disagree with me, but I see my role as looking after the player's perspective. And in that respect, I feel like I haven't changed much.

3.4
Artist Yoshitaka Amano shares the spotlight

Starting with the original *Final Fantasy* games in the '80s, one of the franchise's most distinctive elements has been its promotional and concept artwork from freelance illustrator Yoshitaka Amano, whose pieces for games and other media have made him a celebrity in art circles.

Usually appearing on box art and in marketing materials for *Final Fantasy* games, Amano's work focusses on each game's key characters, presenting them in a fantastical style not typically seen in the games industry.

'I feel like what I add to the

franchise is that my approach differs from a game developer's approach,' he says. 'And I think that gives the art more leeway — it isn't limited to something that would fit into a game.'

While for early *Final Fantasy* games, Amano based his work on pixel art designs and thus had to visualise what those characters should look like in his paintings, on *Final Fantasy VII* he painted a series of pieces inspired by concept art from Square character designer Tetsuya Nomura.

'Amano was way above our pay grade,' says Nomura, who says he likely only met with him once during *FFVII*'s development. 'He wasn't someone we could just talk to casually.'

Yoshitaka Amano

Image illustrator, freelance
Bio on page 226

Because Amano used Nomura's work as a jumping-off point, he didn't have to read between the lines as much to define what the characters should look like before painting them in his style. He says it was a straightforward process and he didn't have any particular advice for Nomura.

'There wasn't really much that I passed along to Nomura-san,' Amano says, 'but I was relieved because I didn't have to do as much.' [Laughs]

Talk to Amano about his work, and he focusses less on the details of each game and more on how the characters make him feel. He can't always describe which characters do what at which point in each game; instead, he looks at the game industry from a high-concept perspective, noting that he sees videogames as a great way to deliver new technology to the masses.

Now in his 60s, Amano says he's less inclined to take on client jobs that come with rigid guidelines, as he doesn't like the limitations that come with that sort of work. But he regularly shows his work at galleries and says he has no intentions of retiring any time soon.

'As an artist, I still feel like a beginner,' he says. 'So there's a lot left to do. I'm going to continue doing this for a long, long time.'

Alexander O. Smith
Localisation specialist, Square US and Japan (1998–2002)
I'm a huge fan of the golden age of illustration, and [Amano] has a real

modern take on that. It really appeals to me, his original work and designs. I actually translated the captions and the essays for a retrospective on his work, completely outside of Square ...

Seeing all the background work [he did later when I worked on *Final Fantasy XII*] was phenomenal. To me, there's a parallel with Tolkien, where you've got a story that – it's a very simple story on the face of it, and there's some words of Elvish in there. And you know, 'Oh, he didn't just make that up. He made up the whole language.' ...

That kind of depth, I think, really comes through in the final product, even if a lot of it gets put aside ... There's so much that's designed and carried out, and a lot of it doesn't get into the game. But I think it really influences everybody who sees it, and I know a lot of the [team looks to it for inspiration]. You know, the art is up on a webdev. During production, a lot of people use the art as their screensavers, so even if the art isn't getting in there, it helps set the mood. So, if your writer's looking at *Beach Volleyball 4* or whatever as a screensaver while they're writing, it's putting them in a different mood than if they're looking at concept art for Ivalice ...

So that kind of extravagant design [that Square embraces], I think, really pays off in the end.

3.5
Composer Nobuo Uematsu tries a new approach

From *Final Fantasy*'s earliest days, Nobuo Uematsu made a name for himself as the series' composer. On Famicom and Super Famicom, that meant extracting distinctive melodies from primitive audio hardware. On PlayStation, all of a sudden, he faced fewer limitations. He could create larger files and use more sounds simultaneously.

'That was the kind of detailed work I did with the programmers, although nobody really seemed to notice that effort,' Uematsu says.

For *Final Fantasy VII*, he says he tried to approach the music like a film soundtrack, worrying less about making a single melody to define the game and more about composing songs that wouldn't overwhelm the game's 3D visuals. 'I tried to make tracks where the melody wouldn't stick out as much,' he says.

As Uematsu tells it, though, composing songs for *Final Fantasy VII* posed a unique challenge due to the nature of the CD format.

Nobuo Uematsu
Music composer, Square Japan

While I was working on *Final Fantasy V*, there were already rumours about the next-generation hardware, but I didn't know what to expect. I'd heard rumours that games were going to be on CD-ROMs, so the first thing that came to my mind was, 'Oh great, now I can hire singers and create tracks with vocals on them.' But I tried it out [for *Final Fantasy VII*] and, even though I had enough space to include vocals, they made it so the game took longer to load between scenes. And I didn't want to do that just for the music, with the game starting and stopping as you play. I didn't think that made sense. So I gave up on that idea and made it work so all the sound would load when you first booted up the game. I was particularly invested in that idea.

Because we did that, though, the sound quality wasn't as high as it could have been. And when the game shipped, I compared the sound quality of *Final Fantasy VII* with another game released around that same time, and the quality for the other title was pretty high. The

Nobuo Uematsu

Music composer, Square Japan
Bio on page 230

game was stopping to load sound data here and there, which I didn't want to do. But after comparing our sound quality with theirs, I thought, 'OK, maybe I should loosen up a little bit and go for higher quality sound even if it hurts the gameplay flow a little bit.' For *Final Fantasy VIII*, we did that ...

I don't remember the specific title I was jealous of, but it was from the *Suikoden* series – whichever title that was out at that time. It loads a lot, and I was thinking that it stopped the game too often, but the quality was really high. That was kind of the trigger to make me think in a different way.

Tatsuya Yoshinari
Programmer, Square Japan
With CDs, the load times were a pain to deal with – not just for the music, but for all aspects of the game. We had to figure out what we could do to cut down on the load times as much as possible. We actually put a lot of effort into making sure the game was constantly preloading whatever players would see next ... We had to kind of cut corners for stuff like that everywhere.

[Note: While working on Final Fantasy VII, *Uematsu composed a song called 'One-Winged Angel' using an experimental approach. It went on to become one of his most popular songs, but he says his goal when he was writing it was simply to get out of his comfort zone.]*

Nobuo Uematsu
Music composer, Square Japan
With *Final Fantasy VI*, I had put a lot of effort into creating the boss tracks. And, since I put a lot of effort in, they turned out really well and gained a nice reputation. After that, I was thinking, 'OK, the normal approach won't exceed what I did for *Final Fantasy VI*.' So a normal tune or classic track wouldn't accomplish much. And I had pulled out 'The Rite of Spring' by the Russian composer Igor Stravinsky, and normally just listening to a track doesn't help me. But I just sat there and kept listening to that track and started thinking I wanted to make a wild, classic tune.

So after that, I started – I would go into the office and just record a couple of phrases that came into my mind. Like in the morning, I would come into the office and record the phrase that popped into my mind. And I just kept doing that for two weeks. And after two weeks, I had a lot of random phrases piled up. Then I took those as puzzle pieces and tried to line them up in an interesting order to make sense as a track. That was a totally new approach for me ... This was the only time I ever used that approach. It was almost like a gamble – it could have turned out great, or it could have turned out horribly ...

That was a really fun time for me since the number of sounds I could use expanded a lot ... That might have been a shift in my career, since I wasn't limited as much any more.

Alexander O. Smith
Localisation specialist, Square US and Japan (1998–2002)
I feel like, more than the changes [Uematsu made in his approach to *FFVII*'s music] – and there were certainly changes – I like the consistency of it. I mean, Uematsu-san's songs sound like Uematsu-san songs, and that's comforting. People want that, especially if it's *Final Fantasy*. It's a real note for the series.

Tatsuya Yoshinari
Programmer, Square Japan
I was a really big fan of Uematsu-san's music. While I was working on the game, Uematsu-san was working on the composition, and he'd send over new tracks as they came along. I actually created a little music player program on my machine just to listen to the tracks he sent over.

Yoshitaka Amano
Image illustrator, freelance
I have high respect for [Uematsu] as a musician. He's a great composer. When you hear his melodies, you can tell right away that he did them and that they sound like *Final Fantasy*. He's even in general music textbooks that you use at school. I think it's great that a game composer was able to become a mainstream success like that.

3.6
Square kills one of the game's main characters

In early 1997, Square wrapped its work on the Japanese version of *Final Fantasy VII.* The team had seen Sakaguchi's ideas through, producing a expansive game with best-in-class visuals, and affirmed the PlayStation as a formidable new platform.

Yet the team had a secret. A spoiler. Toward the end of the game's first disc, villain Sephiroth stabs one of the main characters, Aerith Gainsborough, through the back, killing her.

Looking back, many point out that the scene appears almost comically primitive, with blocky

Tetsuya Nomura

'When a character in a videogame dies, no one thinks it's that sad. They're just characters in a game, after all – you can just reset the game and try again, or you can always revive them somehow ... With "life" as our theme for *FFVII*, I thought we should try depicting a character who really dies for good, who can't come back. For that death to resonate, it needed to be an important character.'

characters and limited animation. But at the time, it stood out as one of the most emotionally charged moments the game industry had produced – a moment that stuck with fans for years. It even made some players cry.

Tetsuya Nomura
Character and battle visual director, Square Japan
Did you know people have been coming up to me for years now and saying, 'You killed Aerith!'?

Yoshinori Kitase
Director, Square Japan
[To Nomura:] Are you trying to blame me for that? [Laughs]

Tetsuya Nomura
Character and battle visual director, Square Japan
OK, so maybe I did kill Aerith. But if I hadn't stopped you, in the second half of the game, you were planning to kill everyone off but the final three characters the player chooses!

Yoshinori Kitase
Director, Square Japan
No way! I wrote that? Where?

Tetsuya Nomura
Character and battle visual director, Square Japan
In the scene where they parachute into Midgar. You wanted everyone to die there!

Yoshinori Kitase
Director, Square Japan
Really? Wait, I'm starting to remember ...

Tetsuya Nomura
Character and battle visual director, Square Japan
Yeah, remember? You and [writer Kazushige] Nojima-san were all excited about this. I was the one who said 'No way!' and stopped you guys. You wanted to kill everyone except the final three characters the player chose for the endgame.

Kazushige Nojima
Scenario writer, Square Japan
Obviously, I'm a scenario writer so I wrote the script where Aerith dies. But, for that decision, we talked it through with the main staff. We talked a lot about how the story would turn out.

Tetsuya Nomura
Character and battle visual director, Square Japan
The theme of *Final Fantasy VII* was 'life,' and we sacrificed Aerith in order to give weight and depth to that theme. Her death is a tragedy but, if we suddenly just killed off everyone else after that, it would dilute the meaning of her death.

Kazushige Nojima
Scenario writer, Square Japan
Back then it was so much easier to change the scenario on the fly. So every day, we'd go back and forth about how to approach things.

Tetsuya Nomura
Character and battle visual director, Square Japan
Long after we made the decision to kill Aerith and the development had progressed considerably, I used to go visit Uematsu-san in his room. Just to hang out and talk about random things. One day, toward the end of development, I visited him to ask him, 'Do you think we did the right thing in killing Aerith?'

Yoshinori Kitase
Director, Square Japan
Really?

Tetsuya Nomura
Character and battle visual director, Square Japan
He said, sure, he thought so.

Yoshinori Kitase
Director, Square Japan
Hah, so casual!

Tetsuya Nomura
Character and battle visual director, Square Japan
I was relieved to hear it.

Nobuo Uematsu
Music composer, Square Japan
When I was playing the game, I was really surprised when she died so early on. Everybody probably thought she was going to be one of the main popular characters, but then she just died right away. Maybe that's the reason why everyone remembers it so much.

Tetsuya Nomura
Character and battle visual director, Square Japan
When a character in a videogame dies, no one thinks it's that sad. They're just characters in a game, after all – you can just reset the game and try again, or you can always revive them somehow. I felt that their lives just didn't have much weight. With 'life' as our theme for *FFVII*, I thought we should try depicting a character who really dies for good, who can't come back. For that death to resonate, it needed to be an important character. So we thought killing off the heroine would allow players to think more deeply about that theme.

Nobuo Uematsu
Music composer, Square Japan
When I was composing [the music that played when Aerith died], I didn't really think about her death, but I felt like she wasn't a very happy character. She was really innocent and pure, but had a tragic kind of life ... I did realise it was probably going to be an important track ...

    If I had known that scene would make people cry, I might have made something totally different – something designed to make you cry. But I went with a kind of sad but beautiful tune, and since it's not the kind of track you typically hear when something tragic happens, maybe that worked out well. When something is missing, people tend to use their imaginations. So since the track doesn't express 100 percent of the feeling in that moment, people might have filled in the gaps in their heads. Maybe.

Tetsuya Nomura
Character and battle visual director, Square Japan
[It wasn't my goal to make people cry with that scene.] It was more wanting people to understand what it means to hurt and to feel a sense of loss.

3.7
Square chases the Western market

Given *Final Fantasy*'s track record, Square executives in Japan didn't have much concern over whether *Final Fantasy VII* would sell well locally. And it did, racking up more than two million units in its first week there, eventually going on to sell more than four million for the PlayStation in Japan.

North America and Europe were another story. At the time, Japanese role-playing games had a cult following in the West, and the *Final Fantasy* series had struggled to expand beyond that small-but-loyal audience.

So as *FFVII*'s Western release approached, Square closed its existing sales and marketing office in Washington and hired two game industry newcomers to start a new office in Costa Mesa, California, giving the company and the series a fresh start in the West.

Yoshihiro Maruyama
Executive vice president, Square US
At the time, more than 95% of the revenue for Squaresoft came from the Japanese market. The remainder five percent came mostly from the US, but maybe one or two percent from the European operation. But the majority of the revenue was from the Japanese market. So they wanted to increase their business outside of Japan. That's how I was hired.

Jun Iwasaki
Vice president of marketing, Square US
I knew [*FFVII* publicity producer] Shinji Hashimoto at Square from my time at an ad agency in Tokyo, and one day I got a call from him and he said, 'Are you interested in moving companies?' So I asked him about it. He said, 'We have a big project coming up, *Final Fantasy VII*, and we want it to sell worldwide.' Then he said he was looking for someone to run marketing for the US market. And I said, 'What? US market?' Because I couldn't speak English well. [Laughs] But he said, 'It doesn't matter. If you're interested in it, please contact me.'

Yoshihiro Maruyama
Executive vice president, Square US
My first assignment at Squaresoft was relocating the Squaresoft operation in Redmond, Washington, down to California.

Jun Iwasaki
Vice president of marketing, Square US

This was sort of the right timing, because Square had shifted from Nintendo to Sony. Square previously had an office in Seattle as Nintendo was nearby. But Sakaguchi-san decided to close the Seattle office, and everyone working there left.

Yoshihiro Maruyama
Executive vice president, Square US

Sakaguchi-san was opening [a] development studio [originally known as Square LA and later Square USA] in Marina del Rey [to work on other projects], so we opened the publishing office [somewhat nearby] in Costa Mesa.

Jun Iwasaki
Vice president of marketing, Square US

Normally, San Francisco would have made sense because Sony would have been nearby. But at that time we were in Los Angeles, and we had a small office inside Sony's US headquarters because *Final Fantasy VII* received the first-party treatment. We controlled marketing but asked Sony to do the budget and publishing and those kinds of things.

Tomoyuki Takechi
President and chief executive officer, Square

Final Fantasy VI didn't sell very well outside of Japan, and so, when we were bringing *Final Fantasy VII* overseas, I was thinking I needed to change something – we needed to do something different. So I was thinking, 'What would make a difference for the game outside of Japan?' ...

The Sony brand was well known around the world, so I was thinking it would be great if it came out under that Sony brand ... Japanese RPGs had a small market outside of Japan. People didn't think of them as high-profile games. And I thought having it come out under the Sony brand would help that perception.

Yoshihiro Maruyama
Executive vice president, Square US

I think it was the third year of the PlayStation. They were still struggling to compete with Sega and Nintendo in the US. And, compared to Sega and Nintendo, Sony's first-party portfolio was rather weak. So, once we decided to [develop *FFVII* on PlayStation], Sony really strongly asked for the publishing rights to Square titles in America as well as in Europe.

Jun Iwasaki
Vice president of marketing, Square US
Yoshi and I didn't have a lot of experience. Sony aggressively pitched to Square to bring *Final Fantasy* over, and at that time Sakaguchi-san and everybody thought we should.

Tomoyuki Takechi
President and chief executive officer, Square
They were really eager to publish it under their brand. And because they were so eager, they also signed a deal with very good conditions where Square earned almost as much money as if we had published it ourselves.

Kyoko Higo
Assistant marketing associate, Square US
For the States, it was a six-title deal [starting with the fighting game *Tobal No. 1*, then a package deal for the next five]. So the first six titles that came out with the Squaresoft label, or logo, they were all published by SCEA and also SCEE.

Tomoyuki Takechi
President and chief executive officer, Square
Sony also agreed to co-promote and market the game around the world. They put in a lot of money, as did Square, and it turned out to be a huge marketing campaign.

Yoshihiro Maruyama
Executive vice president, Square US
Sony's philosophy was they didn't want to market the hardware; all the marketing budget should be for the titles. So once we gave the publishing rights to *Final Fantasy* and others to Sony, they spent lots of money promoting the *Final Fantasy* franchise in America. I think it was a good thing, because they spent so much on promotion – on TV and print and all that kind of stuff ... I think maybe tens of millions ... That was a huge amount at the time.

Tomoyuki Takechi
President and chief executive officer, Square
Just in the North American market, we probably spent more than $20 million on marketing ... Including Europe, probably $30 million ... Including Japan, probably $40 million.

3.8
Final Fantasy VII becomes an international hit

Despite pumping tens of millions of dollars into *Final Fantasy VII*'s marketing, some at Square weren't convinced the game would be able to reach a wide audience in the US and Europe, given the limited reach of previous *Final Fantasy* games. A Japanese RPG had never broken through in the West, and some thought one never would, as they were paced more slowly than popular Western action games.

Iwasaki, Maruyama and the team in Square's new US sales and marketing office took this as a challenge.

Jun Iwasaki
Vice president of marketing, Square US

After I joined Square, Sakaguchi-san mentioned, 'Your mission is to sell a million copies of *Final Fantasy VII*' in the US because, at that time, Sony hadn't reached a million for any title. A million was the magic number.

Tomoyuki Takechi
President and chief executive officer, Square

When *Final Fantasy* was on Nintendo platforms, the series wasn't very popular outside of Japan. *Final Fantasy VI* only sold about 400,000 copies in America ...

[However, with *Final Fantasy VII*] I was very confident that we could sell 2.5 to 3 million in Japan, so that made me comfortable enough that the game didn't seem like a huge risk. But I was also thinking about what it might sell around the world, and I felt some risk there. As time went on, I was able to sign the deal with Sony to put it out under the Sony brand in the US and, because of that I was thinking, 'Oh, maybe we'll be able to sell a million outside of Japan.'

Seth Luisi
Associate producer, Sony Computer Entertainment America

Really, a lot of it was about, 'How can we help bring Japanese RPGs to North America and really show it as a really big triple-A seller?' Because at the time, having worked on Japanese RPGs before, people saw it as a very niche market in North America. They didn't see anything as being able to sell more than 30,000 or 50,000 units. So [with] *Final Fantasy*, our big goal with that one was really to change that. To really promote it as a big title, get the right advertising behind it and getting the really good push behind it so that it had all the attention it deserved and was able to be well received in the North American market.

David Bamberger
Senior product manager, Sony Computer Entertainment America

Our mantra was, 'Don't drop the baby.'

Kyoko Higo
Assistant marketing associate, Square US

The internal office rumours were that if we didn't succeed with *FFVII*, they were going to shut down operations. So in a way, it's like, 'OK, our jobs are on the line,' even though we had this six-title publishing deal. [Laughs] ...

I think the biggest challenge was it visually spoke wonders, but if you were not familiar with the *Final Fantasy* series at all up until that point, and then it came with the number seven, it was kind of like, 'How do we [explain that]?' ... [It was] visually stunning, the best game that you could ever own, etc. All these quotes are out there. But it was more of what's really on the inside. Like, 'How do we communicate that?'

Jun Iwasaki
Vice president of marketing, Square US
We asked Sony not to mention the word 'RPG' because people thought role-playing games were too long and repetitive and had a lot of waiting around. From a marketing perspective, we saw that as a bad word.

Chris Ansell
Project manager, Sony Computer Entertainment Europe
Even the whole turn-based nature of the game was, for most European console PlayStation 1 gamers, like, 'What is this? Why is it so slow?' So we constantly were telling people, 'Look, it starts to feel really fast and just as stressful as a real-time combat game, but you have to get into it. You have to give it a chance to breathe and to teach you the system.'

Kyoko Higo
Assistant marketing associate, Square US
For a game at that time, released during that holiday period, I think a lot of people would agree that it was one of the most beautifully made and presented games. And so, having still images printed in magazines would not have been enough to kind of show how attractive and how appealing it is. I think it was almost a no brainer that we had to look into a TV solution. And Sony was already on board [with doing TV commercials].

Jun Iwasaki
Vice president of marketing, Square US
Sony did some PR and other things. But from a creative point of view, we held the rights to approve things. So I would always send things to Sakaguchi-san to check, because these characters were like his kids. [Sony vice president of marketing] Andrew House always complained about that. [Laughs]

David Bamberger
Senior product manager, Sony Computer Entertainment America
We had a three-month window. So in packaged goods, if you can release

in September, you can get a second reorder for December, and then by Q1 that's kind of the show. The parade has passed.

Kyoko Higo
Assistant marketing associate, Square US
We were getting, I think, weekly updates on pre-orders at that time ... And the numbers kept on going up. And then the ads started to hit and everything was sort of coming together. I'd go into a store, not doing store checks, and see the [marketing on display], the big Cloud standee at the local Electronics Boutique. And a lot of our QA testers ... were also [UC Irvine] students, because UCI was a 10–15 minute drive from our office. And I remember going into our kitchen or lunchroom, and they were talking about how their friends at school were getting super excited and starting to talk about the game. So there were those small moments.

I think the big moment came when it was released and all these cover stories were out. I don't remember how many covers we secured, but I'm sure it was – I remember *PSM*, *EGM*. Most of the magazines wanted covers. So we were starting to see them framed in our office. And then, with week one sales, week two sales, we started seeing numbers. We were hearing ... that this title was on track to become the fastest title to reach a million units in that year. Which we did. We hit it in just under three months.

Jun Iwasaki
Vice president of marketing, Square US
I remember Andrew House called me and said, 'Oh, we shipped a million.' And I called Takechi-san first. And I said, 'We got it to a million!' And he said, 'Oh, that's good.' [Laughs]

David Bamberger
Senior product manager, Sony Computer Entertainment America
I had a $20 bet with [Sony vice president Phil Harrison that the game wasn't] going to sell through a million by March. And I lost the bet.

Tomoyuki Takechi
President and chief executive officer, Square
When we found out that we reached a million [in the US], we all went to Roppongi [a district of Tokyo known for its nightlife] and partied. We were really happy with how the sales were growing and growing outside of Japan. Basically, we went with Sony because we wanted to create titles with a lot of CG in them and make games that were different from what

Kyoko Higo

'After working so hard, long hours, a couple
overnighters even – not just a couple, but many,
overnighters for even someone like myself who
was on the marketing side ... That was, I think,
our proudest and happiest day that came right
before the holidays.'

was already out there, and that's why we made a big investment in *Final Fantasy*. And because of the success of *Final Fantasy VII*, we were able to put out more and more titles after.

Kyoko Higo
Assistant marketing associate, Square US
So it came out on September 7th, '97, and then I remember the first week of December I walked into the office one morning and [Iwasaki and Maruyama] wanted to gather everyone and announce that we had just hit the one-million unit mark, and that Andy House had just sent us a few bottles of champagne, I believe. [Laughs] And [Iwasaki], because he got the news before he left the house, or as he was coming into the office, he bought a few more bottles, and that day was like the happiest day at the office. After working so hard, long hours, a couple overnighters even – not just a couple, but many, overnighters for even someone like myself who was on the marketing side ... That was, I think, our proudest and happiest day that came right before the holidays.

Jun Iwasaki
Vice president of marketing, Square US
Then Kyoko [Higo] and the team gave me a plaque. I was crying at that time, so I remember that. [Laughs]

Kyoko Higo
Assistant marketing associate, Square US
I can never speak on behalf of the development team, but I think it was a huge boost in confidence, in terms of not just accomplishing something, creating this massive game with tons of people, but also to sort of crack that overseas market and being able to have [what we now call] a Western audience or Western fans.

Tomoyuki Takechi
President and chief executive officer, Square
It ended up selling three million in North America and two million in Europe, so it worked out really well. It basically became a worldwide series.

3.9
Final Fantasy VII stirs up controversy

While most aspects of *Final Fantasy VII*'s Western release proved successful, the game didn't come and go without a dose of controversy – one surrounding its portrayal of black and gay characters.

In 1997, players didn't have social media platforms to voice complaint – as they would have years later – but some fans still expressed their distaste for how one of the game's primary characters, Barret, plays into black stereotypes, and how the game's main character, Cloud, visits a bath house filled with men acting out gay stereotypes.

Some of the complaints focused on the game's content – such as Barret's character design, which presents him as a hulking, tough, angry black man – while others focused on its English localisation.

Keith Boesky
President, Eidos (1997–1999)
Well, there was the Barret stuff ... There was the controversy around Barret's language, that he was speaking Ebonics.

Alexander O. Smith
Localisation specialist, Square US and Japan (1998–2002)
I probably wasn't as aware of those issues then as I hope I am now. So it didn't – I mean, I thought, 'Why is this Mr T?' ... That did strike me. I remember that.

Kazushige Nojima
Scenario writer, Square Japan
I don't want to talk about this in too much detail, but personally maybe I didn't put enough thought into [the black and gay stereotypes], into how they would be received. I kind of learned from the reaction I got. Especially with the racial discrimination, I wasn't very aware of what I was depicting in the scenario, and it wasn't until someone told me about the criticism that I became fully aware of what I was putting into the story.

Tetsuya Nomura
Character and battle visual director, Square Japan
I did hear complaints about Barret. I later asked why ... I think it had to do with the localisation and translation not being very good. Ever since that experience, we've paid a lot more attention to localisation. Back then, we weren't very strict about controlling it. We just let the translators do what they thought was best. But it led to them adding and portraying things

Kazushige Nojima

Scenario writer, Square Japan
Bio on page 228

that we never intended in our original script. So since then, we've worked with the translation team to make sure the localisation is as close as possible to the original.

Jun Iwasaki
Vice president of marketing, Square US
Before then, the development teams in Japan [didn't] care about localisation, but after *Final Fantasy VII*, a lot of the teams asked about cultural and localisation issues.

[Note: Apart from the game's controversial elements, FFVII's localisation featured a number of lines that fans found humorous – such as, 'This guy are sick', which went on to become a famous internet meme. Team members credit these hiccups to limited localisation resources, noting that a single staff member working in Square's US office wrote most of the game's English text.]

Chris Ansell
Project manager, Sony Computer Entertainment Europe
Translations are like that – you're always going to have language purists who are like, 'It could be so much better'. And it turns out, well, specific phrases could have been better. But to hear them speak, it's like the whole thing, it should be like a children's book or something in its translation quality. [Laughs] So I do recall there was definitely some feedback about, 'It could be so much better in this language,' or 'They missed the idea of this because I can speak Japanese and you didn't get across that concept.' So there was certainly an element of that, but I do think a lot of it is tough to avoid.

Alexander O. Smith
Localisation specialist, Square US and Japan (1998–2002)
I mean, obviously there's really, really bad translation out there, and *FFVII* is not that at all. What I saw was there seemed to be a lack of flow between some of the lines. Occasionally things would throw me for a loop. They still kind of throw me for a loop. Now I understand why the choices were made better ... I heard [product development coordinator Michael Baskett] only had like a couple of months to do it.

Kyoko Higo
Assistant marketing associate, Square US
[It] was a tiny localisation department ... But without their work, a lot of what we ended up playing would not have happened.

Alexander O. Smith

Localisation specialist, Square US and Japan (1998–2002)

[When working on *Final Fantasy VIII*,] the thing that I heard most in terms of reaction was, 'We're going to spend a lot more time on this translation than they spent on *VII*.' Because they weren't given time on *VII* ...

That's really the story of Square in those days. It's changed a lot now ... There was so little communication between dev and localisation. Localisation didn't even exist as a department back then. We were actually officially subsumed to this – oh my God, what was it? It was like an IT division or something ridiculous. It had nothing to do with localisation at all, except that one of the programmers from IT was the guy that they roped into handling the single-byte character conversions and stuff like that ... You know, they were using GameSharks to hack *FFVIII* so they could get to the text because nobody would give them files. Because, 'Oh, you need files to do translation?' That was news to the dev team at that point. So that sort of complete lack of communication was emblematic of those days.

3.10
Taking *Final Fantasy VII* around the world

After locking in *Final Fantasy VII*'s English script, Square and Sony looked externally to translate and localise the game for release in other territories.

For the French, German and Spanish versions, they hired translation agency SDL from Maidenhead, a town in Berkshire, England. Sony had used SDL before, but *FFVII* proved especially complicated due to its complexity and Square's secretive nature that required the translators to work without seeing the game or having a full understanding of the story.

Gloria Broadbent
Project manager and Spanish translator, SDL
They organised initial testing at the SDL offices here in Maidenhead, where I live. But it didn't go very well ... because they didn't send a complete build of the game. There were some discussions in the background and Square was very, very careful about not releasing the code of the game. So they said, 'Well, I'm sorry but we are reluctant to send the whole build. [If they need that], we will need to then ask the testers to come here.'

Veronique Raguet
French translator, SDL
We had to translate using special software made by them ... And we had real trouble because we had bits of sentences and we had no idea who was talking or what the context was, so we were translating really blindly. And that's why after a while I guess they realised – they must have realised; it was not just a whim. So then they organised for us to go to Japan, on their site, so that we could check all the [lines in the game itself] ...

[Unfortunately, I couldn't go, so one of the other French translators went in my place.] I had a friend coming over and she was coming for the exact two weeks that we were going, so I decided it was not really fair on her.

Gloria Broadbent
Project manager and Spanish translator, SDL
So we went to Japan. This was in '97. August '97. The French translator, the German translator, myself and one of the engineers from Sony. We flew to Tokyo. It was all pretty much paid for by Square.

We had an absolutely amazing time. They booked the Dai-Ichi at Meguro, which was this amazing hotel next to the Imperial Gardens. We were just having a bit of a luxury life. But the work was very, very intense ... What we were told at that time was that if you have to play the game from beginning to end, going through all the different variables, or most of the variables, it would take you solidly – I mean full-time – three months. But obviously we couldn't stay for three months. That would be too much. So they asked us to test the critical parts, which was going to take two weeks, or 15 days.

So that was the time that we stayed and, well, I don't know how familiar you are with Japanese life, but they do work very hard. Basically, we would start every day at around 10 in the morning and we never stopped before midnight.

Of course, we had breaks for lunch and usually a very late supper, at night, but obviously we were not playing the game. What they organised – and this was fantastic, I thought – [was] they had very young kids that were absolutely wizards with the game, and they were [playing] the game, you know? So I was sitting next to one of them who was playing the game in Spanish. Obviously, the same for my colleagues, French and German. And we were going through all the different bubbles with the dialogues and the stories and everything ...

So that took us two weeks. We did this solidly for two weeks ...

[Then] as we were leaving at midnight pretty much every night, we used to go for dinner and obviously we wanted to go to a sushi bar or a place like that. I remember more than once we went into a sushi bar or restaurant that was open. Everything is open at that time; it's like Russia at midnight – lots of people very drunk.

The strange thing was that [since] we were three girls, they would not have us in the same room as the men were. There was a room at the back of the restaurant and that's where we were. We were not allowed to stay in the same room as men. There was a lot of [discrimination] at that time. Now it's probably different in Japan; I haven't been since that time. But it was this very clear discrimination of women, men. And I was always [wondering], 'How does this happen in restaurants?' In many restaurants, it happened to us.

But it didn't happen in the office. The attitude at work was very different.

Aftermath

4

4.1
Square ports *Final Fantasy VII* to PC

In the period following *FFVII*'s initial release, Square shuffled the staff who had worked on the game. Some continued on to the direct follow-up, *Final Fantasy VIII.* Others moved to help with Square's additional titles. Others teamed up with Western publisher Electronic Arts to form a new distribution partnership. Still others went off to start a new studio in Hawaii, which caused problems for the company as time went on. It was a time of change for the company riding high on *FFVII*'s success around the globe.

One smaller project to appear in the aftermath was a *FFVII* PC port.

Even before the PlayStation game's release, a small group in Square's Costa Mesa office began looking into the possibility of porting the game to PC. Square wanted to reach players in the US and Europe who didn't own PlayStations, and its publishing deal with Sony didn't prevent it from pursuing a PC version elsewhere. After some back and forth, Square struck a deal with *Tomb Raider* publisher Eidos.

Many at Square saw this as an experiment, figuring the company might be able to squeeze extra sales out of the game it had put so much money behind. An experiment that began with a phone call between Square US head Yoshihiro Maruyama and Eidos president Keith Boesky.

Keith Boesky
President, Eidos (1997–1999)
I got a call two weeks before E3 from Yoshi. I'd never met him before … I got a call from Yoshi just saying, 'Hi, this is Yoshi Maruyama, and I'd like to set a meeting at E3 [the Electronic Entertainment Expo] because we'd like to talk about publishing *Final Fantasy VII*.' And I'm sitting in my office, and I just – I looked at the phone. I said, '*FFVII* – are you serious?' And he said, 'Yeah.' And I said, 'OK, I'll be there tomorrow'. And I got on a plane and flew from San Francisco to Orange County to meet with him, because we didn't know what it was going to be, but there had been a ton of press.

Yoshihiro Maruyama
Executive vice president, Square US
[A lot of publishers in America and Europe didn't realise what we had with *FFVII*.] Another publisher referred me to somebody who was covering their Asian operations. I won't name the company, but … [Laughs]

Keith Boesky
President, Eidos (1997–1999)
I was just, 'OK, I'm there'. EA wouldn't take the meeting … Pretty much nobody else. There were a couple other people who took meetings at E3, but I was the only one who went down. I met him in Orange County. I don't even think he showed me anything. And we talked about it. We told him we were interested. He came by. He met some more people at E3. E3 was in Atlanta that year. Met more people at E3. And then he went for six months and visited all of the Eidos offices, which is more than I did as president. But he went to Hamburg. He went to France. He went to all the offices to look at Eidos' operation.

Elaine Di Iorio
Manager of business development, Square US
My understanding was it was kind of an experiment. [Square] had never done a PC port and they thought that they would set up a team in the US to do the PC port ... So we made the rounds [to find a publisher].

Yoshihiro Maruyama
Executive vice president, Square US
Eidos was a very exciting company at the time because *Tomb Raider* was becoming a big franchise. And they did tremendous marketing.

Frank Hom
Associate producer, Eidos (1995–2001)
We had our act together in some parts. We were making it up as we go in other parts. But the product was always number one.

Elaine Di Iorio
Manager of business development, Square US
I thought it was a great company ... From a business standpoint, they just seemed to have everything we needed. They understood us, Square and the game. They were a small company, so they were a little more lean and a little more agile ... It wasn't going into some larger company that we might get lost in.

Keith Boesky
President, Eidos (1997–1999)
It was Dave Cox, Paul Baldwin and Mike McGarvey and Sutton Trout who launched *Tomb Raider* in November of 1996 and made us the number two publisher in the world, only behind EA. So those guys are good. They knew what they were doing. *Tomb Raider* was a great game, but great games don't [sell without marketing] ...

But it was iffy. It was a risk ... We were kind of on the fence because, first of all, would somebody play a *Final Fantasy* [asynchronous] RPG on a PC, and then also, would people play an async RPG on a PC that's coming out a year after the console [version]?

Elaine Di Iorio
Manager of business development, Square US
I think releasing a PC version was a big risk, but it was also kind of a test. I don't think [Square] was expecting the same kind of triple-A title that they got on the console, but I think they wanted to kind of try their hand at the PC version and see what would happen.

Frank Hom
Associate producer, Eidos (1995–2001)
All the producers [at Eidos] were huge fans, and we completely support-
ed the idea. Especially me – I was very excited, super happy. Like, 'Oh,
we've gotta do this no matter what.'

Keith Boesky
President, Eidos (1997–1999)
[Maruyama] wanted $1.8 million. And you have to understand *Tomb
Raider* cost $900,000. So [that] was a lot of money for a title at the time
– and was a lot of money for PC. And I walked down the hall, and Mike
McGarvey was in town. McGarvey ran Europe; I ran US. And we went into
Rob Stannett's office, who was the CFO ... and Mike picked up a piece of
paper off of Rob's desk, wrote down a million eight ... And he just looked
at it and said 'OK, yeah, that's about 100,000 units.' And 'Rob, what do
you think?' And Rob said, 'Yeah, we can do that and just move on. Let's
not be stagnant over the decision.' And that was it. That was our green
light, and we picked it up ...

That [$1.8 million] was the MG, minimum guarantee ... It's an
advance against royalties. We had a royalty deal with them where we
published and we gave them a piece of every unit we sold, less certain
deductions, and I don't remember the details of what they were. And the
advance, what happens is you give them a forecast: 'I think we'll sell this
many. And we'll back that up by giving you hard dollars, non-refundable,
up front against the earn out.' So we wrote them a cheque for $1.8 million
as a minimum guarantee to secure the publishing rights on PC ...

We signed a deal about six months after the first meeting,
which is record time for a Japanese company.

Frank Hom
Associate producer, Eidos (1995–2001)
It was a pretty high-profile title in our company, equal to *Tomb Raider* at
the time. It was just a big deal.

William Chen
Lead programmer, Square US (1997–2000)
We had about 15–20 people working on it, mostly in Square's Costa Mesa
office but with some help from Tokyo.

Yoshihiro Maruyama
Executive vice president, Square US
It was much more work than we thought [it would be]. Because PC was –

148

it was very tough to decide what kind of CPU the game was going to run on, with what kind of graphics card ... We spent lots of time fine-tuning the technical level of detail.

Frank Hom
Associate producer, Eidos (1995–2001)
It was a huge risk on the development side, because the team had to do a lot of work. Almost, I believe, 80 percent of the game code was rewritten. They took a very custom-made game for the PlayStation, and they had to extrapolate that and redo a lot of things to make it just work on PC ... I actually camped out there for a while because it was getting delayed.

Keith Boesky
President, Eidos (1997–1999)
It was a very complex port. Because there were, if I remember, there were five different game engines.

William Chen
Lead programmer, Square US (1997–2000)
Square had different people writing code for each part of the PlayStation game, with different styles and engines, so it was quite a challenge to unify those on PC with a small team. But overall I'd say the development went better than expected, and the game sold much better than we all expected as well.

Keith Boesky
President, Eidos (1997–1999)
I think we forecast 100,000 units and we did a million plus.

Yoshihiro Maruyama
Executive vice president, Square US
[I remember it being] 200 in North America, 200 in the European market, and 100,000 in Korea.

Frank Hom
Associate producer, Eidos (1995–2001)
It sold pretty close to a million at full price, I would say, and then it went into a number of variations – budget versions and whatnot.

Keith Boesky
President, Eidos (1997–1999)
I think the first royalty cheque we sent them, and Yoshi will never ac-

knowledge this, but he did this because I joke with him a lot about it ... The first cheque we sent them, I think, was $2 million. That means, in the first quarter, we exceeded the million eight, plus another two million in royalties. So we did real well. And Yoshi sent the cheque back to me ... I get this cheque on my desk, and I called him up and said, 'What are you doing?' And he says, 'You didn't include a royalty statement so we couldn't accept the cheque.' And I said, 'Yoshi, you're dealing with an American company. Keep the cheque. Ask for the statement, but don't send it back to me' ...

It's funny because the deal actually led to us becoming very close to merging Square and Eidos. The way that we saw it was, our philosophy of game building was very similar. Neither one of us did licensed [intellectual property]. Both of us were focused on very, very high-quality games – high-quality, character-driven games. And we had Europe and the US and they had Japan. And we actually had the first meeting at that E3 in Atlanta, and then the second E3 in Atlanta, we had a meeting [with] the CEO of the holding group, Charles Cornwall, Ian Livingstone, the chairman of the company, and then Miyamoto – the owner of Square, not Miyamoto the Nintendo dude – and then the owner of Digicube, which was a division of Square. We had a big, private dinner and came really close to a merger in '98 [but Square decided to go another way] ...

The funny thing is, I got a call [a couple of years ago] from Square, because they wanted to re-release the PC version, and they asked me if I knew where the gold master was. [Laughs] I left the company in 1999. What am I gonna do with that? 'Oh yeah, you know, it's right here in my desk drawer. That big box that I carried out? Yeah, I was carrying the gold master and all the source. Let me just give it to you.' Yeah, they lost it.

Frank Hom
Associate producer, Eidos (1995–2001)
My understanding is actually – what I'm most kind of proud of – is that they kept the code. I believe the version that they put out on mobile and PS4 is actually the PC code that we worked on.

4.2
Square teams up with Electronic Arts

While Square ended up making money with *Final Fantasy VII* PC, the company's bread and butter remained PlayStation games. And after working on six games with Sony, Square's US publishing plans – on both console and PC, including those for the company's next big game, *Final Fantasy VIII* – were up in the air.

Some within Square's US office wanted to begin to publish games themselves. Others wanted to continue working with Eidos. Square Japan's executive team had a different plan – teaming up for a distribution deal with Electronic Arts.

Together, the companies formed Square EA as a joint venture to publish Square's games in the US, and EA Square to publish EA's games in Japan.

Jun Iwasaki
Vice president of marketing, Square US
After we finished the Sony deal, the first-party deal ... I thought we finally had a chance to be a publisher of our own in the US. But all of a sudden, headquarters ordered the joint venture with EA. It was a tough time.

Yoshihiro Maruyama
Executive vice president, Square US
EA came very strongly to us. They wanted the rights to the PC version [of *Final Fantasy VIII*] ... They negotiated really hard for the PC rights. Because, you know, we gave the [*Final Fantasy VII* PC] rights to Eidos, and Eidos did tremendous work. So I felt it was right to keep giving the licence to Eidos but, you know, we started having the joint venture, so ...

[Note: Eidos ended up publishing FFVIII *for the PC in Europe, while Square EA did so in the US.]*

Tomoyuki Takechi
President and chief executive officer, Square
When we first released *FFVII* outside Japan, we had Sony's help, and we realised that you need strong distribution to succeed outside Japan. And we were wondering if we should go solo or partner up with somebody. And then Miyamoto-san suggested, 'Why don't we become partners with EA to put out our games outside of Japan?' So we went and talked with EA.

Jun Iwasaki
Vice president of marketing, Square US
I don't know why the executives at that time decided to form Square EA. I think it was some sort of political issue.

Keith Boesky
President, Eidos (1997–1999)

[My guess is they did it because] in dealing with Japanese companies, historically there's a concept in Japan of 'famous.' And EA is a famous company, and Eidos wasn't.

Frank Hom
Associate producer, Eidos (1995–2001)

We were a new publisher, kind of a hip, new publisher, but we weren't the known-name, stable publisher, and that was EA at the time. And I think [Square's] president in Japan decided, 'If we're going to do a long-term commitment, we're gonna do it with somebody a little more established and not new,' even though the US office group really liked us.

Rex Ishibashi
Vice president of business development, Electronic Arts (1997–2001)

Electronic Arts had more of a track record, not that this was on the table, but [of] acquisitions and partnering, than I think Eidos did. And I think it's safe to say it was a much healthier company financially ... Certainly a spark plug in the whole discussion was the success of *Final Fantasy VII*.

John Riccitiello
President and chief operating officer, Electronic Arts (1998–2004)

[*FFVII*'s success] was all of the reason for wanting to do it. It started with [conversations about wanting] to publish and/or distribute *Final Fantasy* and it grew into this [joint venture] ... I mean, realistically, when you stand in a room with another smart person, you've got an idea, you listen to their ideas, and you settle on one that works for both people. Square had global ambitions and wasn't willing to sort of cede control in a traditional publishing deal. So we structured something different.

Rex Ishibashi
Vice president of business development, Electronic Arts (1997–2001)

There were two joint ventures – one joint venture set up in Japan where the idea was Square would help EA, and a joint venture set up in North America where EA would help Square. Obviously the biggest clear opportunity, and proven opportunity, was for EA to take over distribution of *Final Fantasy* and the other Square games in the West. Whether EA had games that would truly, or could truly, crack Japan was another matter.

John Riccitiello
President and chief operating officer, Electronic Arts
(1998–2004)

There's no question that the Western deal worked a lot better. EA didn't make a lot of content that worked in Japan, culturally, and realistically no Western publisher did. Oddly enough, back in those days it was really unusual for a Western title to get more than 50,000 units in Japan. And so I don't think that really got off the ground in a huge way. But it was actually never the bigger part of this deal to begin with. It was just reciprocal because two big companies like to imagine they're reciprocal. It was really more about the Western deal and the marketing of *Final Fantasy*. I don't have the unit numbers in front of us, but they were pretty damn good.

Rex Ishibashi
Vice president of business development, Electronic Arts
(1997–2001)

It certainly wasn't perfectly smooth sailing. At the end of the day, Square – even with its US presence – was a very Japanese company. And again, when I say that, I say that respectfully. I don't mean a big hulking dinosaur like Matsushita or Honda. I mean kind of a new breed of Japanese company that was very aggressive ... And there wasn't a long history of creative Japanese companies cracking the West as Square was doing, at least in terms of videogame unit numbers. There just wasn't. You can point to things like *Godzilla*, or whatever you want to point to, and they're kind of really novelties, right? You can point to Kurosawa films, and 90% of the film-going public in the West has no idea who he is. So, long way of saying, it was certainly interesting because, while Japanese games companies were very successful in Japan, of course, there weren't many independent companies, certainly besides Nintendo, that were really making headway in the way that Square was with the *Final Fantasy* franchise.

John Riccitiello
President and chief operating officer, Electronic Arts
(1998–2004)

I'd say if there was a downside [to Square EA], it was probably a more complicated structure than you needed for what amounted to a publishing deal.

Shinichiro Kajitani
Vice president, Square USA

Each quarter we'd have board meetings, and we'd meet with [Electronic

Arts CEO] Larry Probst and John Riccitiello. But we didn't really see eye to eye and had a lot of different opinions on a lot of things, so there was a lot of friction there.

Jun Iwasaki
Vice president of marketing, Square US
I worked with John Riccitiello. We had quarterly board meetings, and we always fought in those. Maybe he hated me. [Laughs]

John Riccitiello
President and chief operating officer, Electronic Arts
(1998–2004)
It was trivial. I mean, first off, the most senior person that was working on the deal [at Square] in the US would have been a junior manager at EA. They were young and inexperienced ... There was a guy, Iwasaki or whatever, at that point. He was also a pretty junior guy, and a good guy – nothing wrong with him. And they always wanted higher volumes and bigger guarantees, and the [EA] sales guy in the US wanted to be a little more conservative and let the market play itself out. You know, the standard friction between somebody that's responsible for the outcome and someone that's responsible for a better forecast. There was definitely a little bit of friction ... If you were taking a look at 'the battlefield,' it would look peaceful and harmonious from 30 feet in the air. But, in the foxhole or under the table, some of the children were foot-fighting a little bit, I guess. But it was never much more than that, really.

Rex Ishibashi
Vice president of business development, Electronic Arts
(1997–2001)
You know, any time there's a joint venture of two very powerful, creative, opinionated companies that have had success in their own right, I'm not surprised that there would be disagreements. Especially when you think about cultural differences. We're talking about two companies that, I think, at every board meeting required a translator ... I very specifically remember, in the early conversations, where we were trying to use a third-party translator to conduct some of the conversations. And Yoshi Maruyama's English is better than my Japanese, but he and I would be correcting the nuance of the translator. Because it was like, 'That's not quite right'. You know, you take that literally and you're going to be making decisions based on the wrong information, or the wrong communication.

Yoshihiro Maruyama
Executive vice president, Square US

Square was focusing on PlayStation only, whereas EA was a multiplatform game company. They kept publishing on Nintendo as well as Sega as well as PC. So there was a bit of a different approach because they could spread out marketing across different platforms, but you know, we only published for the PlayStation. So there was that kind of discussion between us – why were we just doing it? [Laughs] We told them that the Japanese game market was always a 'winner takes all' type of market. It used to be Nintendo. Now it's PlayStation, so we had no intent to make any games for other consoles like Sega or Nintendo. But the US market was twice as big. So they understood it, but they still wanted us to make games for other consoles. Which Square, you know, firmly refused.

Shinichiro Kajitani
Vice president, Square USA

Probably the biggest thing was, EA and Square were really frustrated with each other because, at the time, EA didn't think that Japanese RPGs would sell in the States at all. And conversely, Square didn't think that EA's games, just by localising them into Japanese, would sell in Japan either.

Jun Iwasaki
Vice president of marketing, Square US

I never understood Square EA ... After we finished the EA deal – so five years after – finally we did our own publishing in the US ... When we did that, we made huge profits compared to previous years.

John Riccitiello
President and chief operating officer, Electronic Arts
(1998–2004)

It was never intended to be forever. You know, so, it worked out nicely. I don't think there's any hard feelings either way ... Partnership worked out. EA made revenue and profit. Square made revenue and profit. Square brands got better established in the West. And I maintain a relationship to this day with Square. It's a very positive one.

4.3
Square makes a *Final Fantasy* movie

Of Square's post-*Final Fantasy VII* initiatives, many say the most ambitious was its studio in Honolulu, Hawaii, which the company opened in 1997.

While Square had multiple studios around the world, the idea behind the Hawaii studio was that it wouldn't just develop games. It would also make movies. As Square had ramped up its CG resources working on cutscenes for *FFVII*, Sakaguchi saw the potential to push that technology further.

The first result of that idea, *Final Fantasy: The Spirits Within*, was a big-budget film loosely

connected to the rest of the *Final Fantasy* series. The movie hit cinemas in 2001.

Kazuyuki Hashimoto
CG supervisor, Square Japan; chief technical officer and senior vice president, Square USA

Toward the end of *Final Fantasy VII*, Sakaguchi-san came to visit my desk and said, 'Oh, we have a lot of movie clips in *FFVII*. We may be able to make a movie now.' And I said, 'Are you serious?'

Tomoyuki Takechi
President and chief executive officer, Square

After the success of *FFVII*, there were two main things that changed, two main goals that we set for ourselves. The first thing is we wanted to put a lot of power behind our graphics capabilities, because we were thinking in five or 10 years that was going to be the big thing in games. That was one of the reasons why we decided to make the *Final Fantasy* movie. Then the second thing was we knew that network features were going to be a big deal, so that's why we decided to take *Final Fantasy* online [with *Final Fantasy XI*].

Kazuyuki Hashimoto
CG supervisor, Square Japan; chief technical officer and senior vice president, Square USA

You know, when Sakaguchi-san asked me to join Square, I told him that if Square was thinking about just competing with Sega or Namco, I wouldn't be interested. If Square really wanted to compete with Disney or other global entertainment companies, then it would be very exciting.

Jun Iwasaki
Vice president of marketing, Square US

This was Sakaguchi-san's dream. He wanted to make the first 3D graphics movie.

Tomoyuki Takechi
President and chief executive officer, Square

In some ways, Sakaguchi-san had a lot of flexibility to do what he wanted after *FFVII*'s success, but Square wasn't just his company. Square was a very ambitious company, and as a digital entertainment company, we were talking about wanting to be bigger than Disney. So we were thinking, 'OK, what is a digital entertainment company? What's the definition?' And then we came across the idea of, 'We're not just a company that makes games. So why don't we make movies as well?'

Kazuyuki Hashimoto
CG supervisor, Square Japan; chief technical officer and senior vice president, Square USA
Right as we finished *FFVII*, Sakaguchi-san asked me to build up the movie production studio in Hawaii. Most people at Square had one month off, a one-month vacation. I didn't. [Laughs] I needed to work on this movie project. I got involved with the Hawaii studio from the very beginning, to find office space, until the lease ran out. So I was there from the very beginning to the very end. The whole time was about five years, 1997 to 2002.

Shinichiro Kajitani
Vice president, Square USA
Sakaguchi-san, he left for Hawaii and built a studio in Honolulu and, from that point on, he had nothing to do with Square's games in Japan any more. He just concentrated on making the movie.

Motonori Sakakibara
Movie director, Square Japan
Officially, the reason for Hawaii was that we could connect all the artists from Japan and America, and Hawaii is the middle point between both countries ... [But we moved there] because Sakaguchi-san liked Hawaii.

[Note: When the movie hit theatres, it was a critical and commercial failure. On the aggregate site Rotten Tomatoes, it earned a critic score of 44% and an audience score of 48%. Team members credit the reaction to three things: the story not appealing to a Western audience, the characters looking realistic but not like recognisable stars, and the release being close to 9/11. Some also note, though, that challenges behind the scenes played a role in the end result.]

Kazuyuki Hashimoto
CG supervisor, Square Japan; chief technical officer and senior vice president, Square USA

Kazuyuki Hashimoto

CG supervisor, Square Japan; chief technical officer and
senior vice president, Square USA
Bio on page 227

We needed to decide how to build the movie production. Game production is like a small-scale factory, but movie production needs to be a large-scale factory ... Not easy. [Laughs] You know Pixar? They spent about 10 years to build a movie pipeline in their studio. Square did it in just two years.

Junichi Yanagihara
Executive vice president, Square USA

Whenever you make a movie for the first time, there is a learning curve ... And sometimes, as you can imagine, there is what we call 'development hell' in which many different people come in and try to give so much input that it causes a delay of the process. As a result, we couldn't reach the consensus as to what to do with the story.

Kazuyuki Hashimoto
CG supervisor, Square Japan; chief technical officer and senior vice president, Square USA

Working in the game industry [in Japan, we were used to] working until very late at night ... Many of the people were from the US or other nations, and they'd prioritise their personal lives. They wouldn't stay at the office so late. Usually they would go home at seven or eight at the latest. Things were all different.

Steve Gray
Vice president of game production, Square USA

That movie project you could tell was going to be fucked ... It ended up being unbelievably expensive. It was very cool, right? Especially for the time, it was pretty amazing. But, you know, [normally when you make a CG movie] you storyboard things out and you try and be very, very careful about only building the things that you're really going to need, because otherwise it gets crazy expensive ... I was talking to Sakaguchi and to the guys who were bringing in the producers and saying, 'You know, you can't just start building. You've really got to think about this and make an animatic.' And they were just like, 'Oh, no. We're just going to build the whole city and then we'll like fly around with the camera and see what we like.'

Hiroshi Kawai
Character programmer, Square Japan

The checks and balances weren't there. I think, in terms of producing a game, Sakaguchi-san was probably pretty reliable in terms of his beat in terms of what worked and what didn't work. But when it came to working in a different medium, I think ... the fact that there wasn't really anybody there to provide objective and constructive criticism was a detriment.

Alexander O. Smith
Localisation specialist, Square US and Japan (1998–2002)
The movie ... was an unmitigated disaster ... I talked to the lawyer, and I just remember at a party, but she was the lawyer from Hawaii who had handled their applications for doing the movie there. And there were so many tax benefits on the table, and they didn't take a single one. Because they went in and they were like, 'We're bringing our team'. And they were like, 'You hire 10 percent Hawaiian and you get this huge tax cut.' And I don't think it was like Sakaguchi sitting there going, 'No, we're keeping it pure. It's our team.' I don't think there was any thought at all. I think it was like, that came in and the whole organisation was so dysfunctional that, when that kind of news hits the grind, it never gets to the person that needs to hear it.

And that's the problem when you've got that kind of power structure. It's like a family thing. And this is endemic in Japanese companies where it operates like a family instead of a business. And so, if something isn't on the family's radar, it just doesn't happen. And there are so many missed opportunities there. So apparently, they could have saved so much money – millions of dollars – if they had taken advantage of these really easy [opportunities]. They just had to hire janitors locally, really, and they could have done it.

Yoshihiro Maruyama
Executive vice president, Square US
I think [*FFVII*'s success] changed [Sakaguchi's] style in a slightly negative way. [Laughs] He thought he could do anything within the company. That's why he started investing even more money in *Final Fantasy* the movie, which became one of the biggest flops. That made him a little out of control. The original budget of the film was like $40 million dollars, and it [ended up costing] close to $150 million. So when I actually did the calculation on how much it was going to cost based on the number of people Sakaguchi wanted to assign, I quickly figured out it couldn't be finished for $40 million. But you know, they did it anyway. They kept investing more money.

Hiroshi Kawai
Character programmer, Square Japan
There's sort of this expression in Japan where you say, 'It's somebody else's money.' And you can take it as, 'You need to treat it with respect

because it's not yours.' Or you can say, 'Well it's not mine, so it's there to spend.'

Junichi Yanagihara
Executive vice president, Square USA
It was all funded by Square itself. It was self-funded. And sooner or later, if you study and analyse this, you'll probably run into some articles about what happened ... After the film project, Square went through a financially challenging time.

[Note: The Spirits Within *wasn't the Honolulu studio's only project. Square's efforts in Hawaii extended to a short film for* The Matrix *spin-off compilation* The Animatrix *and the development of the games* Parasite Eve *and* Final Fantasy IX. *The Honolulu studio also became a sister studio to Square LA, at which point both adopted the name Square USA.]*

Shinichiro Kajitani
Vice president, Square USA
We had about 240 people in Honolulu and about 80 people in the LA studio ... We had to go around and tell everyone, 'Sorry, but we're going to have to ask you to leave.' Right at that time, [Yoshiki] Okamoto at Capcom headhunted me so I went to work there instead.

Tomoyuki Takechi
President and chief executive officer, Square
With the money we earned from *FFVII*, we decided, 'OK let's use half of it as an investment for the future, and let's save the other half.' So, because of that, we didn't go into a management crisis when the movie underperformed ... From a business point of view it wasn't a success. But I feel like a Japanese game publisher in the year 2000 creating a movie in CG was a big accomplishment, so I don't regret making it at all. I think it's something that people will come around to praise in the long run.

4.4
Sakaguchi leaves Square and the company begins to change

Following the struggles of *Final Fantasy: The Spirits Within*, Square ran into another issue: the company delayed its next major game release, *Final Fantasy X*. While games industry delays are common and the company had plenty of smaller projects to keep things moving forward, the combination of two big financial setbacks so close together put Square in a tough position.

Eventually, both Sakaguchi and Takechi left the company.

With the departures of its top creative and business figures,

Square – for many – began to feel like a different company.

Tomoyuki Takechi
President and chief executive officer, Square
In 2001, the fiscal year ending in March, that was the first year that Square ever went into the red ... The movie was the main reason for that. But we also delayed *Final Fantasy X* past the end of the fiscal year, and that was another big factor ... And to take responsibility for going into the red, I decided to step down and leave the company. Then Sakaguchi-san said, 'Well, it's not fair for you to have to leave, so I'll take responsibility and leave as well'. That's why Sakaguchi-san left.

Hironobu Sakaguchi
Producer and executive vice president, Square Japan;
chairman and chief executive officer, Square USA
There were many, many reasons why I left. [Laughs] But to try and sum it up ... My official title was executive vice president, and that meant, of course, that I had a mountain of administrative tasks to attend to. Every morning I would have a stack of papers waiting on my desk to review and approve. If there was a change to the labour laws, for instance, I had to go through training and then update our employee policies. There was a ton of work like that, but I wanted to be involved in creating things again, so all this stress was just building up in me. I really loved Square, you know, and I was grateful for my position, but it just didn't feel like me. That feeling was the main reason I quit.

Tetsuya Nomura
Character and battle visual director, Square Japan
For me, it was like, 'Huh? What happened?' [Laughs] There was a generational difference, you see. There was Sakaguchi-san's generation, then there was Kitase-san's generation, then below that were younger guys like me. And we didn't have that much direct contact with the older guys ... It took a while before anyone even told me he had quit! I think I was one of the last people to know. I remember how, when I came into work that day, everyone had this sombre look on their face.

Alexander O. Smith
Localisation specialist, Square US and Japan (1998–2002)
Personally, I was like, 'Oh, end of an era,' you know. But I didn't feel like
– because so much of the time I was there, and I hate to come back to
this yet again, but it was the movie. And so, it didn't seem like such a bad
thing. And certainly the guy's got more stories left in him. It didn't seem
like that was the place to tell them.

Kazuyuki Hashimoto
*CG supervisor, Square Japan; chief technical officer and
senior vice president, Square USA*
I left Square because Sakaguchi-san left. I had a position in the Tokyo
office, so I could have gone back [after the Honolulu studio closed], but it
felt like the company had changed a lot.

Tetsuya Nomura
Character and battle visual director, Square Japan
I shouldn't be saying this, but hmm, how to put this? It was like *Sangokushi* [the Chinese literary series *Romance of the Three Kingdoms*]. You
know, where the king dies, and then a civil war erupts and everyone
starts fighting each other.

Yoshinori Kitase
Director, Square Japan
Let's see, what can I say here? At the time, Sakaguchi-san held a unique
position at Square. He was simultaneously an executive vice president, a
board member of the company and, a game developer himself. There's
no one quite like that in the company today so, in that sense, things did
change a lot.

Tetsuya Nomura
Character and battle visual director, Square Japan
Yeah, Sakaguchi-san had shaped so many different things at Square.
Now there's multiple, different voices.

Yoshinori Kitase
Director, Square Japan
That singular vision kind of changed when he left – as Nomura said,
instead of Sakaguchi-san deciding things alone, when he left, there was a
greater diversity of ideas that flowed in.

Hiroshi Kawai
Character programmer, Square Japan

It's one of those [things] where, when somebody like Sakaguchi-san, who had such authority in the company, kind of just disappears, there's this vacuum that exists where nobody can really arbitrate between your devs and your artists and your game designers. And in that environment, most people – especially in Square – tended to avoid conflict and try to resolve things as best as possible. And, unfortunately, the way each individual tried to resolve it wasn't necessarily in the end user's interests.

Kazuyuki Hashimoto
CG supervisor, Square Japan; chief technical officer and senior vice president, Square USA

Especially during the *Final Fantasy VII* period, Sakaguchi-san made every big decision. That was why everybody moved quickly. It was so exciting. And after Sakaguchi-san left, no one wanted to take responsibility, so all the decision-making needed lots of approvals, which took a long, long time. The company didn't move very quickly. It suffered from 'big company disease'.

Shinichiro Kajitani
Vice president, Square USA

When Sakaguchi-san wanted to make a decision, it would just happen like that. But after he left, several people had to do it ... It became more of a committee-based thing, so it took a lot more time to get things done.

Yoshihiro Maruyama
Executive vice president, Square US

Management was totally changing at Squaresoft. They went from one extreme to the other. Before then, they had no control over costs. But all of a sudden, cost control became a big deal.

Motonori Sakakibara
Movie director, Square

The company seemed like it was becoming [more about costs than creativity]. At the beginning of this interview, I mentioned that Square was very creative – the first priority was creativity, right? But I think after the movie project, they changed some of the direction of the company, especially after Sakaguchi left.

Tetsuya Nomura

'I shouldn't be saying this, but hmm, how to put this? It was like *Sangokushi* [the Chinese literary series *Romance of the Three Kingdoms*]. You know, where the king dies, and then a civil war erupts and everyone starts fighting each other.'

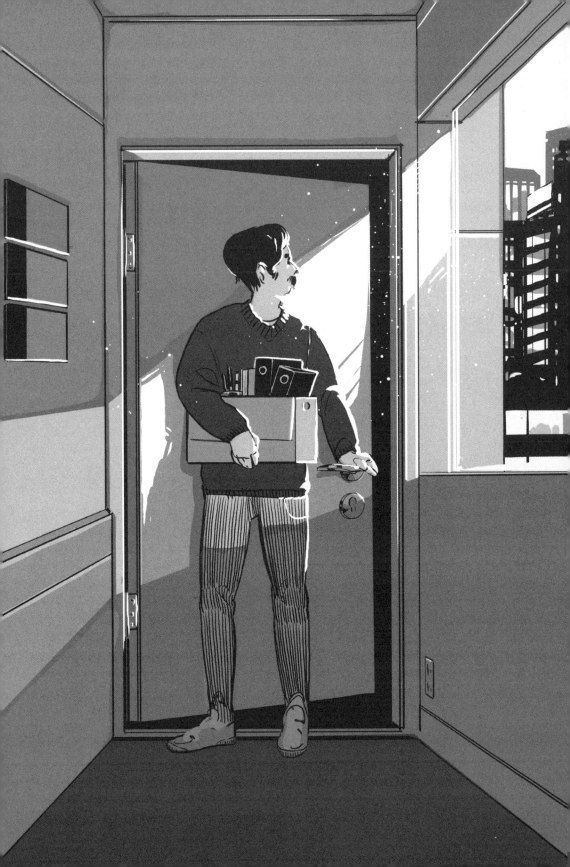

Junichi Yanagihara
Executive vice president, Square USA
It was a big event, the period between 1995 and 2001 ... Everything went by very quickly and very dramatically.

Alexander O. Smith
Localisation specialist, Square US and Japan (1998–2002)
It was the transition from the family business to the business business ... Everything got stratified and there was more division between departments. We had to do – oh yeah, there was all this reporting stuff that went on. Like, 'What did you do this quarter? How did things work out?' That sort of stuff. So yeah, it was a cultural shift.

Tomoyuki Takechi
President and chief executive officer, Square
When I left the company ... things were changing a lot. Personally, leaving the company was, of course, a sad time. But I thought that the company seemed to be headed for big things, so I was happy for it ... I always feel like, if you don't take risks, the flowers aren't going to bloom. So I'm happy things worked out for the company after I left.

4.5
Square makes *Final Fantasy VII* into its own franchise

In the early 2000s, as Takechi and Sakaguchi left Square, and others, including new president Yoichi Wada, took over, Square wasn't only changing behind the scenes. It was also changing its output, as *Final Fantasy* shifted from a franchise with one new sequel every couple of years to a franchise with multiple branches and spin-off titles releasing more frequently.

In 2003, one of these branches took the form of what Square called the 'Compilation of *FFVII*' – a series of a new CG film, *Final Fantasy VII: Advent Children*, and three *FFVII* spin-off games. Some saw this as Square whipping the horse too hard to get more sales out of the *Final Fantasy* brand. Others liked the variety and creativity behind the approach.

Hiroshi Kawai
Character programmer, Square Japan
I think it was important to get somebody [running the company after Sakaguchi left] who had a different perspective on the business of making games. And it's not the actual development of games per se, but to actually be shipping games and selling games.

Yoichi Wada
President and chief executive officer, Square/Square Enix (2001–2013)
When I joined the company in the year 2000, I foresaw that the game industry would get bigger and more diversified, and I knew I'd need to make changes in order to respond to that. So the goals prior to 2000, and the targets Square needed to work on after 2000, were a little bit different ...

One unique thing about the *Final Fantasy* franchise is that, usually if you have a series of numbered games, the protagonist remains the same and you have a central theme that connects the series. But with *Final Fantasy*, every game is different from the last. So, because of that, we decided to create subseries within the overall series. So there's a *Final Fantasy VII* series of games underneath it, and *Final Fantasy X* has its own spin-off games underneath it.

Jun Iwasaki
Vice president of marketing, Square US
I was disappointed because they wore out *Final Fantasy*. I heard after I left the company ... that *Final Fantasy*'s loyalty decreased with US customers.

Alexander O. Smith
Localisation specialist, Square US and Japan (1998–2002)
Well, I mean, it's that problem of you have to balance making money with a known cash cow against diluting the IP. So yeah, well, what are you going to do? I think that's symptomatic of Square. I think it would be awesome if, in an alternate universe, Square could say, 'OK, we're just having 50 people now. Everyone else is going to take a vacation for two years. And these 50 people are going to make a *Final Fantasy* game.' You know, and what happens? What do they do? That would be really cool to see. But impossible. And when the balance sheet is determining everything, then I think you back yourself into that situation where, 'We have to release things.'

Nobuo Uematsu
Music composer, Square Japan
Personally, I want each game in a series to be treated with a lot of care, so I'm not a big fan of one game having a bunch of spin-offs and sequels. But I understand that from a company, sales, money point of view, it makes sense.

Yoichi Wada
President and chief executive officer, Square/Square Enix (2001–2013)
It's true that we had financial reasons for it. When I joined in 2000, Square was on the verge of going bankrupt. And right before merging with Enix, *Final Fantasy X-2* contributed to our overall profit, which was the greatest in Square's history. We were able to go out on a high note. But also from the consumer's side, *Final Fantasy* has great stories and solid characters, and people wanted to see where characters came from and what their backstories were and what happened next. We got a lot of requests from people along those lines, so in some ways we were just responding to those requests ...

One thing I made sure of was that we had the same creators work on each of the spin-offs. So if it's a spin-off of *FFVII*, I made sure that Kitase-san and Nomura-san were the key creators to do it, or else it would turn into a different game.

Tetsuya Nomura
Character and battle visual director, Square Japan
From the beginning, we planned to only do four spin-offs of *FFVII*, and we publicly announced that [the 'Compilation of *FFVII*'] would end with those four. We planned it that way ourselves so we wouldn't oversaturate the market.

Hiroshi Kawai

Character programmer, Square Japan

I think it has a lot to do with how you sort of massage your users' expectation. A lot of these spin-offs – at least my impression [is they came] after the fact. 'Oh, we've spent so much time and so much money creating this, and now we don't have as much. But we left an opening here that we might be able to exploit.'

Frank Hom

Associate producer, Eidos (1995–2001)

I believe, if those games were uniform in quality – some of them were fantastic, and some of them were just mediocre – but I think if they were uniform in quality, people wouldn't be able to get enough. They would want more and more *Final Fantasy*. And I think, even today, people want more and more *Final Fantasy*.

4.6
Square staff reunite at Microsoft

As Square went through changes in the early 2000s, Sakaguchi, Takechi and Hashimoto weren't the only staff to leave. For a company with hundreds of employees, some turnover was normal. Yet it turned out that a handful of team members ended up working together a second time as part of Microsoft's then-newly formed Tokyo studio built to support the Xbox in Japan.

In one chain of hiring, Microsoft brought in Square's Takayuki Suguro, who then brought over Yoshinari, who then brought over Kawai. Along with a handful of other ex-Square employees – such as Maruyama, who took over as managing director of Microsoft Japan in 2003 – some say it felt like a small reunion at Microsoft.

Tatsuya Yoshinari
Programmer, Square Japan
It's not that we were trying to rebuild the team from Square at Microsoft on purpose or build the new Square or anything like that, but I and Sugaro-san and a guy named [Daisuke] Fukugawa and another guy named [Soichiro] Yasui who worked on *Final Fantasy IX*, we all joined around the same time. I guess it was a bit coincidental. And there were a few other people from Square there as well.

Hiroshi Kawai
Character programmer, Square Japan
Personally, I'm an Apple person. You would not find me dead with a PC in my house. I just grew up with Apple, so it's one of those 'hell would freeze over before I would go to Microsoft' kind of things. But considering that there weren't really opportunities that were interesting in Square, and that hopefully, with a clean slate and with Microsoft's expertise in mass-producing software, I'd be able to do something different, I decided to take the leap.

I told Sakaguchi-san that [after I made the decision to leave Square and he was still there], and I guess maybe this was his policy with everybody: 'You can leave me once. I'll forgive you once. But just this once.'

Tatsuya Yoshinari
Programmer, Square Japan
Basically everything was different between Square and Microsoft. But if I had to choose the most significant difference, it was that we didn't [initially] have anyone at Microsoft that was like Sakaguchi-san back at Square, that powerful leader who really kind of had that aura of leadership and drove everyone forward.

Hiroshi Kawai
Character programmer, Square Japan

[For the original Xbox] Microsoft wanted to ship a game that only Japanese people could play, and they had three teams internally. Two of those teams kind of croaked. Our team was essentially on life support until I decided to raise my hand and say, 'I'll take full responsibility.' The title that ended up shipping was *Magatama*. It never got ported over to the States. It's a hack and slash game, nothing special, but we did ship, which I considered, at that time, to be my primary objective ...

At that point in Microsoft Japan, as you can imagine, morale was very low. Two of those three projects did not ship. Teams got canceled. Even feedback that Japanese devs tried to give to HQ wasn't being reflected. There was this big hoopla about the Duke controller that came out initially ...

A lot of people were generally suspicious of Microsoft HQ. But then Maruyama-san came along and he said, 'Don't worry. I'll take care of all the politics.'

Yoshihiro Maruyama
Executive vice president, Square US

I happened to know [Microsoft executive] Robbie Bach from the early days of Xbox. So he contacted me one day and he told me that he was looking for a managing director of the Xbox operation in Japan. I was a little nervous because the Xbox in Japan had been a big challenge. But they told me that the company was committed to keep operating worldwide, including Japan. So that's why I took the job.

[Note: Upon joining Microsoft, one of Maruyama's first tasks was to reach out to Sakaguchi, whom he knew from his days at Square. Sakaguchi had started an independent studio called Mistwalker, built as a small group to oversee and produce games, rather than to do the heavy lifting on big projects. And Maruyama wanted to sign Mistwalker – and the other staff Mistwalker needed – to make new role-playing games for the Xbox 360, in the hope of repeating the success of games like Final Fantasy VII. *This led to the creation of two new games:* Blue Dragon *and* Lost Odyssey.*]*

Yoshihiro Maruyama
Executive vice president, Square US

Sakaguchi was already independent after the, I shouldn't call it, big trouble of the *Final Fantasy* film. So I wanted to bring him back in.

Hironobu Sakaguchi
Producer and executive vice president, Square Japan;
chairman and chief executive officer, Square USA
My first reaction was, 'It's not going to happen.' Maruyama came to my office and he pitched me on the idea, but I wasn't interested.

Hiroshi Kawai
Character programmer, Square Japan
Despite the drawbacks that I knew that Microsoft had at the time, I think Microsoft was one of the few places in Japan that had the financial clout to pull off something of a Sakaguchi-class game.

Yoshihiro Maruyama
Executive vice president, Square US
I went to approach Sakaguchi-san, telling him that Kawai-san was with us. That's why – because of him, I think Sakaguchi decided to work with us.

Hiroshi Kawai
Character programmer, Square Japan
[Maruyama] called me up and said, 'I'm trying to get Sakaguchi-san to come over and work on a 360 project.' And he got us together.

Hironobu Sakaguchi
Producer and executive vice president, Square Japan;
chairman and chief executive officer, Square USA
Kawai was a very talented programmer. I remember I originally flew out to Boston to recruit him to work at Square ... He had joined Microsoft and we met and he said, 'You know, I have a team. I can run a team. I'm already running a team, and here it is.' And that helped change my mind.

Tatsuya Yoshinari
Programmer, Square Japan
It was really kind of a shock, in a good way. Because we had Maruyama-san, Kawai-san, and Sakaguchi-san all together for a game called *Lost Odyssey*. And after moving from Square to Microsoft, I never thought I'd get to work with Sakaguchi-san again, so getting those three guys and some others on this new project, it really was a pretty big deal.

Hiroshi Kawai
Character programmer, Square Japan
I convinced Sakaguchi-san that – it's kind of unorthodox from a Japanese point of view, but from a pure development point of view, Microsoft does

have its assets. They do have their strengths. You just need to under-stand them and work in concert with them. Unfortunately, that 'in con-cert' part kind of fell apart during the latter portions.

Yoshihiro Maruyama
Executive vice president, Square US
I was hoping that *Lost Odyssey* and *Blue Dragon* would come at the launch of the Xbox 360, which didn't happen because of the delays of the projects.

Hiroshi Kawai
Character programmer, Square Japan
So after Sakaguchi-san came on board, we were working on a prototype with a very small team [for the game that became *Lost Odyssey*] ... And trying to get a game engine put together for the 360 developed internal-ly in Microsoft Japan was proving to be very [challenging].

Tatsuya Yoshinari
Programmer, Square Japan
Lost Odyssey was a really difficult project. That was when it really kind of hit home that, with all the new technology we had – and especially with very limited human resource support – it really was difficult to make very nice, high-end graphics. And, at the time, we were working on the Unreal Engine, but it was still kind of in development itself. The game and en-gine were being developed simultaneously, and they both had bugs that needed to be worked out. So what would happen was we would update the engine, and then the game would no longer function, and we'd have to go and work that out and figure out how to match it up with the new-est version and everything. We kind of had to wait for the engine to catch up with parts of the game. So yeah, it took a lot of work, and making the graphics look as good as they could was really difficult.

Hiroshi Kawai
Character programmer, Square Japan
Unreal, in terms of graphics, it's very capable and very, very impressive. But it was still essentially in alpha stage when they were trying to push it onto us ... And even the devs [at Epic], their attitude – I'm not saying this with any disrespect, but it was one of those, 'If you don't like it, don't use it' [situations]. Their devs were very clear from the get-go, saying, 'This is what Unreal is made for, and if it fits your needs, great. If it doesn't, you're on your own. If you need documentation, read the source code. If you need help, write to us in English.' ...

And while we were making a little progress on that front, we were running into personnel issues in terms of trying to hire people. Microsoft has this interesting sort of hiring scheme where, even if you say you had $100 million in your budget, you would be capped to this thing called 'headcount' and it would be completely independent of your budget. So you may only have a headcount for two full-time employees even though you have a massive budget, and you could not increase that. You'd have to essentially trade horses with some other team who's willing to give up their headcount, and even then it's still a precious commodity.

Hironobu Sakaguchi
Producer and executive vice president, Square Japan;
chairman and chief executive officer, Square USA
Even my jaw dropped when I heard about some of the staffing difficulties and having these restrictions. I was like, 'Well, we did say we're committed to creating this next generation RPG and you're talking about doing this with 30 people? How could you?' So there were some surprises for me as well.

Yoshihiro Maruyama
Executive vice president, Square US
We couldn't use Microsoft employees to complete the projects because their overhead was very expensive. So we had no choice but to create a separate company ... It was a paper company just to hire developers.

Hiroshi Kawai
Character programmer, Square Japan
So it came to this point where it was like ... we just weren't going to get the people we needed within Microsoft, so it would be better to spin the team off into a separate company. But creating a company from scratch would be risky, so we would like to have somebody 'sponsor'. And that's where they found Cavia, who was willing to take the team on and sort of be a sibling of our team. [Even then] it was very difficult to convince people to move over.

So despite having this new company ... we were just calling it NewCo at the time, before it became feelplus – and although we had this shell of the company to work with, we still couldn't get our devs. And I don't know who got wind of it first, but ... there was a role-playing game that was being developed by a company called Nautilus, who was a subsidiary of ... Aruze, who was primarily into pachinko games in Japan ...

I think they were no longer interested in maintaining that team. They were saying, 'If anybody's interested in taking this team on, we're here to listen.' And they had a full dev team there, and the dev team had been making role-playing games at that point. So the powers that be thought, 'Hey, why not just combine those guys with existing Microsoft guys and we now have double the capacity, so look out.'

Well, unfortunately it didn't, because the guys from Nautilus – I guess they were kind of given the cold shoulder. I mean, they were essentially being kicked out on the street, although they didn't end up being on the street because we picked them up so quickly, but they were kind of treated that way, so they were very suspicious of the guys from Microsoft. And especially the devs were absolutely not interested in using Unreal. They were saying, 'You cannot trust code written by a third party. We have no idea what's in it. We won't be able to customise it.' Yadda, yadda, yadda. So we have 10 engineers from Nautilus, 10-plus engineers from Microsoft, and they're not talking to each other.

[Note: After many political ups and downs, including multiple role changes and joining the development team at feelplus, Kawai decided to resign.]

Hiroshi Kawai
Character programmer, Square Japan
It had gotten to a point where it had taken a toll on me physically ... My day-to-day work cycle was I would go [to the office] one day, sleep overnight, and then stay at the office until the last train [the next day]. I would only go back home once every two days. And it was just getting to the point where – the [Tokyo Game Show] demo that we shipped, I just, my body was going to fall apart or something else was going to fall apart. So I said, 'I will get the TGS demo done. I will get it to the point where you can build upon that and finish the game. But after that, I just cannot do this job.'

Hironobu Sakaguchi
Producer and executive vice president, Square Japan;
chairman and chief executive officer, Square USA
Kawai had to deal with a lot. I can see why he remembers that and how that could have been one of the most challenging things that he went through.

Tatsuya Yoshinari
Programmer, Square Japan
It was really difficult working in that environment with two separate teams and hierarchies because the management lines weren't clearly set

187

as far as who reports to whom, and who's whose boss and everything. For example, Kawai-san, who had been my boss at Square, went over to feelplus, and basically, for the first time, he was no longer my boss. And that was pretty strange, that this guy who had been my boss for a while suddenly wasn't any more, even though I was still working with him. And even though he technically wasn't my boss any more, the guy who was in place as my manager wasn't really exactly the best fit for the job. So to be honest, deep down, I never really considered that guy to be my boss. I trusted Kawai-san a lot more ... So yeah, it was a bit difficult working with two separate teams and two separate hierarchies with really kind of vague and not very clear-cut management report lines.

Hiroshi Kawai
Character programmer, Square Japan

During *Lost Odyssey*, it was very difficult working with [Sakaguchi], not only because he has his own style of getting things done [but also because of the culture at Microsoft]. It wasn't important just to get that game out. It was important to get their employees to develop themselves, and maybe this is going too far by saying shipping something was a side effect, but it kind of felt like that at times, being a manager at Microsoft. And that conflicts very, very much with the way that Japanese games tended to get developed, where you'd have this sort of authoritarian, almost dictator-like director at the very top who not only handled creative decisions but also handled HR decisions and had full authority there. It just didn't work that way at Microsoft.

Hironobu Sakaguchi
Producer and executive vice president, Square Japan;
chairman and chief executive officer, Square USA

My rule is that I don't want to put out anything that's not complete. You know, I'm not going to put out anything that's half baked or even like 99%. It's got to be in a state and a condition where I'm fully confident. And then, even after it goes out, I want to go back and play the game and be sort of surprised by what my team and I put into it. So whatever it takes to make sure that we hit that quality bar, it's going to go in there ...

It was a very challenging project. Unexpected things would come up and there were things that we just couldn't resolve purely from a technical standpoint. And there were some staffing issues on the Microsoft side. But, if I look back in time and if I were to be fair to, you know, all of my projects, even going back to *Chrono Trigger* and *Final Fantasy VII*, I think most of them have been equally challenging.

I think of it like when someone is in labour. Sometimes they have a very quick and easy time. But, for most of my games, we tend to be in the room for hours trying to get these things out.

Hiroshi Kawai
Character programmer, Square Japan

I didn't talk to [Sakaguchi] when I finally decided to leave. But I did get an email from him [later on] saying, '*Lost Odyssey* shipped, and maybe we could have a chat over drinks.' Because I guess maybe he felt guilty. Maybe he wanted to get things sort of out in the air. At that point, I was just kind of tired and I declined.

Epilogue

B

Everyone goes their separate ways

In the years following *Final Fantasy VII*'s release and aftermath, Square went through a multitude of changes – merging with its former rival Enix, acquiring publishers Taito and Eidos, and turning over hundreds of staff members. From the *FFVII* team, Kitase, Nomura and Naora stuck around, while most of the rest of the key figures moved on, many of them landing in high-profile roles in and around the game industry.

Uematsu went on to become one of the industry's most acclaimed freelance composers, working on personal albums and games like mobile RPG juggernaut *Granblue Fantasy*.

Amano continued his freelance work and became one of the most popular artists in Japan, selling some new mainstream works for six figures while dabbling in occasional games industry jobs.

Sakakibara and Yanagihara started Sprite Animation Studios, a CG production company focused on animated films and shows, such as *Pac-Man and the Ghostly Adventures.*

Hashimoto helped Electronic Arts with early PlayStation 3 research, co-founded game studio Avatar Reality with *Tetris* overseer Henk Rogers, and later took a senior position at NVIDIA.

Nojima went freelance, working on stories for games such as *Super Smash Bros. Brawl* and

Dragon's Dogma Online, in addition to numerous *Final Fantasy* titles.

Iwasaki started boutique publisher XSEED, then took over GungHo Online America, the US branch of the company behind Japanese mobile chart-topper *Puzzle & Dragons*.

Yoshihiro Maruyama became an agent, connecting developers with clients, and working with staff from Square such as high-profile writer/director Yasumi Matsuno.

Kajitani went to Capcom and Game Republic before taking a senior position at development team/graphics tech company Silicon Studio.

Luisi oversaw the creation of

the *SOCOM* shooter series at Sony, and later founded independent studio Impulse Gear to develop the PlayStation VR shooter *Farpoint*.

Sakaguchi, meanwhile, went on to run his concept team Mistwalker, overseeing a variety of console and mobile role-playing games – even one published by Nintendo in certain territories, *The Last Story*.

Looking back, Sakaguchi says *FFVII* marks a personal career highlight, though not one that eclipses the others he's seen over the years. Asked if he thinks his career changed course because of *FFVII*, he says: 'I hear that a lot, but to me the change didn't feel so sudden. The game was very successful, but really

Yusuke Naora

'It was a *Final Fantasy* full of so many firsts, and I still love the fact we challenged ourselves to the fullest in every aspect – the world, the designs, the execution, etc. Given the technical constraints of that time, I have no complaints.'

it felt like part of the momentum we had been building since the first *Final Fantasy*.'

He also admits to sometimes playing out hypothetical alternate scenarios in his head.

'I do wonder sometimes what would have happened if we'd just stayed in 2D and put a lot of effort into another 2D game instead,' he says. 'And if we didn't go with PlayStation, what would have happened? What would the next *Final Fantasy* have been? It seems like a big question mark. I don't know. The series took a completely different direction with *FFVII*, so that's the only *Final Fantasy* we know after *VI*. But in an alternate universe, there could have been a different approach. That's something that I still wonder about.'

For many on the team, though, *FFVII* stands out as not only a successful game, but a standout moment in their careers, a rare case of resources matching ambition at a turning point in the game industry.

A game that fans may even discuss 500 years after its release.

'It was a *Final Fantasy* full of so many firsts, and I still love the fact we challenged ourselves to the fullest in every aspect – the world, the designs, the execution, etc.,' says former Square Japan art director Yusuke Naora. 'Given the technical constraints of that time, I have no complaints.'

Outtakes

C

Alexander O. Smith joined Square while *Final Fantasy VIII* was in development, and went on to become one of the company's most popular localisation editors – both while working there, and in his post-Square freelance career.

On his knowledge of Square before applying to work there:

It's funny. I'm going to get myself in trouble here, because I had very, very little knowledge of Square. I hadn't played a single *Final Fantasy* game – I knew it existed. I played games. But I was entirely Mac-based, and Apple II before that. So *Wizardry*, *Bard's Tale* and then *Civilization* and shit like that all through college. And the console thing – my parents didn't let me have a console, so my console experience growing up was going over to a friend's house and playing *Zelda* and that sort of stuff, *Mario Bros.*

I don't know what the timing was, but I think it was after I decided to apply for the job. I saw the job was out there and I said, 'Well, I probably should play one of those games.' And I put in *Final Fantasy VII*, which is the last one that had come out. And played – I don't think I actually finished it. I was in grad school, so I didn't have a ton of time. And I had a *Civilization* addiction too ... I played *FFVII* about halfway, I think. And my impressions were, 'Yeah, this is amazing'. I mean, the visuals were just amazing. And I loved the idea that storytelling games had come so far. Because I'd been playing *Wizardry* and *Bard's Tale* and stuff like that, and they're the story of *Zork*. You know, it's got a story but it's really just dressing on the gameplay. Whereas this was actually trying to sell the story as the main reason you wanted to play the game.

So you know, I had fun. Fun playing the game. And [from what I saw of the translation, I thought I could bring a different viewpoint to it]. So ... I'll try to get this job because it looks like I have something to add here. And I hadn't done any game work at that point, but I'd done a lot of translation already. This was grad school – I was in a PhD program, actually, for classical Japanese literature. And I had been in Hawaii for a year before that for undergrad. And when I was in Hawaii, I started subtitling soap operas – 'home dramas' as they're called – for the local Japanese television [station] – KIKU Television – and then they would resell those to the international channel in the States.

So I had some translation experience, and subtitling actually turned out to be really, really useful because this was still the era of – well, I know we're back in the era of – but it's the character limitations, because you can't fit so much on the screen. Which were loosened and loosened and loosened. Of course, now everything's mobile, and we're right back where we started to incredibly tight character restrictions. But the subtitling experience helped a lot, I think, in understanding the problems involved. You know, 'You've only got this much space to work with. How are you going to get a story across?'

On filing off rough edges:

Creation by committee just can kill so much. So many good ideas get destroyed. That's always been sort of one of my pet peeves. And we had it in localisation too. We would have meetings where we would go down through glossary items on like, 'What are we going to call this? What are we going to call this?' And it's nice that you do develop essentially a style guide, a working style guide, without actually having to sit down and write a style guide. But at the same time, you lose out on a lot of crazy ideas, because if one person in the room thinks it's ridiculous, it's not going to happen. And you know, different personalities react differently to that kind of situation, but it can kill a lot of creativity. And I think that probably happened on many levels at Square. The more meetings you have ...

On working with Yoshinori Kitase:

He always struck me as extremely pragmatic. Not one of the big ego guys, so that makes him really easy to work with. He was always really aware of localisation issues too, which I think – you know how you can tell a lot about someone by the way they treat their waiter? I feel like the way that a dev person treats localisation is very similar. It's sort of like the litmus test for, 'Oh this guy's the asshole.' Or, 'This guy doesn't care.' They might care about quality in one area, but they might not care about quality across the board. Or they just don't understand, and they don't care enough to try and understand. And so, localisation in general across the board is seen as a service industry or, in the worst case scenario, the black box that you feed stuff into and it shoots out the other side. And so yeah, you do get that kind of attitude of, 'Well, we made the game. You just do your thing and get it out there. Why are you trying to change stuff?' Never got that from Kitase.

On Square's California offices:

They moved the office in LA from Costa Mesa to [El Segundo] right by the airport. The reasons given for that were to be closer to Sony people and because of the airport it was a lot more convenient. But they apparently couldn't sell off the old building space, so for a stupid-long time they were paying for both offices, which is – I guess they could do it at that point, but that sort of stuff depletes the war chest.

While much of this book focusses on *Final Fantasy VII*'s creation in Japan and marketing success in the United States, the game was also a breakout hit in European territories. Chris Ansell worked for Sony Computer Entertainment Europe's marketing department right as *FFVII* was getting off the ground.

On how he got to Sony in the first place:

I was born and raised in Sydney, Australia, and first job out of university was with Sony Computer Entertainment Australia, which had, I think, four employees at the time. I called them and I was so excited for PlayStation 1 and I knew it'd be big, so [I said], 'Do you need any interns? I know all the games.' They said, 'Yeah, we'd love to have you.' So I went and basically put my name on every single folder and file I could for that week, and tried to make myself as invaluable as possible, and they realised they needed someone to basically rep the games locally for PR, for Australia. So I basically got a job as a junior PR assistant and, from that, kind of moved through the ranks of marketing in Australia and, within a year, was asked to go to London headquarters to be a product manager ...

For me, going to London was like, a second university. It was incredible. I was like 23 at the time and just loved it. Obviously PlayStation was emerging and it was super exciting times. So the very first project I was asked to handle, to market, was this game I'd never heard of. It was called *Final Fantasy VII*.

On the European marketing approach:

We really pushed the scale of the city and used the city a lot in the imagery. From memory, I think it was more about the characters in the North American marketing. I think [there were always] some healthy differences of opinion between Sony Europe to Sony US. I'm not sure if that's still the case but, obviously, they both have very separate markets to serve. I know that we loved pushing the scale and the scope of the city. It was just an incredible graphic. I know that the [point of purchase] posters we designed – Square in Japan loved them. They were just absolutely in love with them.

I do remember one funny instance where part of the image was flipped to make the design work best and we didn't realise, of course, the kanji written on the smoke stacks was also flipped ... So, thank goodness, we caught that at the last second working with Square and we reversed it, but little stresses like that were kind of par for the course as you're working, you know, across cultures.

On the European box art:

The pack shot we did was just the logo, and in North America it actually was Cloud in front of the city. So that was a huge difference ... Generally, most of the covers on the pack shots had to be very explanative – what the actual game experience, moment to moment, would be like, you know? Like the *Doom* pack shot, for example.

So just putting the logo at the time, I recall it was very risky. There was a lot of talk about it. Like, 'Should we do it? Should we maybe just copy the American style and just have Cloud in front of the city with a sword and make it more straightforward?' But the European territories came back and they all loved the boldness of it. It just felt very confident. You know, almost as if you were saying this game is going to be so big, we know all we have to do is show our logo ...

And it really paid off, I think. You know, we kind of continued down [that path]. I also did the marketing for *FFVIII* and so we carried on that tradition of just the confident logo, center stage, on the white background. [I] love white pack shots because white stands out and it's what the eye immediately gravitates to first on the shelf. EA's sports packaging is always white. There's a reason for it. And so, just on shelves, it was instantly noticeable.

On the game arriving late in Europe:

You didn't have the internet at any state like it is today, so there was no real upwards communication feedback loop. People were dying to play this thing and obviously there were a lot of Japanese imports but of course, you know, you had to speak Japanese. So it was an issue but we knew that a quality translation was super important ... It takes time. It was the biggest game that Sony QA, Europe team, had ever experienced.

I recall conversations about the cycles for doing a complete QA pass on every single fresh revision build that came in – it was significant time. So when you're planning out your logistics and your CD production timelines at the Sony disc manufacturing plants, it all had to be very carefully planned for and extra QA people brought in when needed, just to make sure we hit the dates for the European launch because it was just so much text, so much of a big game to get through to do quality QA passes.

I do recall, yeah, obviously there was a lot of talk about 'Do we get the US version? Do we import the Japanese version?' From the fans – you know, from the fanbase that we could pick out. Our key message was to make sure that everyone knew it was going to be absolutely worth the wait to get the best version in their language.

On office space in Tokyo:

Getting to work with the Japanese team was incredible. For me, it was a real eye-opener culturally as well. Just seeing how an office is laid out in a large Japanese development studio versus a European development studio was kind of a [shock].

Generally space is at a premium in Tokyo, so I noticed that the workers back in the office, back then, were kind of working in the equivalent space of a phone box. You know, a very cool-looking phone box but imagine like a honeycomb looking down on an office. It was like that and that was incredible. I'd never seen an office laid out that way but, obviously, they had so many people working on the game. It was like, 'Wow. What an interesting sort of layout here.'

On game developer celebrities:

[I was fascinated by] the reverence for, obviously Sakaguchi-san and Nomura-san. [It was] incredible just seeing people of this stature in Japan and how ... Japanese gamers and press would be around them. It was like, 'Wow.' [It was] for me at the time, the nearest I'd felt to being near a movie star. So that was really fun just to witness, you know? The sort of, the incredible presence these guys had, given their accomplishment.

After graduating with a computer science degree from MIT, Hiroshi Kawai worked as a programmer on *Final Fantasy VII*, *Parasite Eve* and others. But as he tells it, he started at Square in a different role.

On how he got hired at Square:

Square was looking for translators. And although it wasn't a programming position, I figured, 'Well, if I can get my foot within the door and if they find out that I can actually code, maybe they'll let me code.' ... This was Square Japan. I was still back in Boston at the time. I had an interview and the people who interviewed me were Yanagihara-san, Sakaguchi-san and Kajitani-san. And it wasn't really quite an interview ...

They came out to Boston, though my suspicion is it was really a shopping trip for the Sakaguchi family in disguise. You can quote me on this if you want to, because I actually had to take part in one of those hiring trips later on myself, to sort of act as a translator. And you know, Sakaguchi-san would be out during the day, nowhere to be found, and he'd be coming back with a bunch of shopping bags. So he did something.

But, after I passed the translator's test, I think Sakaguchi-san didn't really give me any signal in terms of whether or not they were interested, but a little while later they sent me a letter saying, 'We'd be interested to have you join, and we'll wait for you to graduate,' because it was still my junior year at that time. And upon graduation – I actually didn't graduate during the June season because I had to finish up my thesis. So I ended up coming in September of 1994 ...

[Then once I got] to the office, I actually found out that they hired me as a game designer. They never bothered telling me. They were just, 'We want to hire you.' And I thought, 'Hopefully they'll consider my programming skills.' But it turned out they hired me as a game designer. Or actually, Sakaguchi-san said, 'We've got this weird guy, Japanese guy who's been living in the States for a long time. He knows a little about

Japanese culture. He might make an interesting game designer.' So that was the logic, as far as I knew.

On the early days of file saving:

There was no centralised backup mechanism that existed at Square. I mean, even bulletin boards where you share ideas – when I joined Square, it was so low-level where it was essentially a file server where you copied a file off, you wrote to it and then you uploaded it. And if you realised that somebody else had updated it before you, you'd have to redo it. So it was that primitive at that point. There were no centralised backups. Everybody was working on their individual PCs. Even the notion of version control was non-existent ...

So if there was a catastrophic hardware failure, all that person's data would just completely be lost. And we were fortunate in a sense in that most of the hardware that we had at that time was tentatively pretty reliable. [But] you'd essentially build your sort of little subset module of your code, copy it somewhere, then the lead dev, Narita-san, would copy it from there onto his machine and build it there. And if Narita-san croaked or any of the developers croaked, that portion of the game would just be gone, because there was no way of recovering it.

On *FFVII* lead programmer Ken Narita's programming philosophy:

Narita-san had this philosophy where every single *Final Fantasy* had to be rewritten from scratch. And that was the way they ensured that they refactored bad code [from] the past, and would hopefully be able to add in new features as they were optimising it. But once it starts getting to the PlayStation level ... or even the PlayStation 2 level, that becomes completely impractical to write everything from scratch. In that sense, although *Final Fantasy VII*, *VIII* and *IX* essentially had the same sort of framework where you had the pre-rendered 3D backgrounds for the fields, there was no code that was shared between *FFVIII* and *FFIX* ...

I can understand where he was coming from, but your competition doesn't necessarily play by those rules, and you have to be aware that your competition can one-up you very quickly and very easily. Which became probably more and more apparent as Square was struggling in the PlayStation 2 years ...

Although, in the end, I didn't agree with his development philosophy – and if it hasn't changed, I probably still don't agree with it – he was extremely helpful, extremely supportive in allowing me to be able to do what I was able to do at Square. Without the acknowledgement of his confidence in my ability to do things, I would never have been able to work on *Parasite Eve*, or for that matter work on *Final Fantasy IX*.

On what happened to the SGI hardware bought for *FFVII*:

It was becoming pretty outdated by the time we were working on the latter portion of *FFVIII*, where people started figuring out better ways to get more realism out of the PlayStation hardware and started texturing stuff. And as far as I remember, by the time *FFIX* came around, those SGI boxes were kind of getting old. And at the end of *FFIX*, I think the thinking was they were hoping to be able to take that hardware and use it for the *FF* movie to render stuff, but apparently [they] didn't even find use for it there either. So [the machines] were just sitting in some kind of room.

On *Parasite Eve*:

My involvement happened after I finished *FFVII*, and at that time there were already rumblings of Square LA in Marina del Rey. And growing up in LA myself, I figured it would be great to be able to work in LA. And I remember having a talk with Sakaguchi-san saying, you know, 'I'd like to go to work in LA.' He said, 'Well, you've only finished one game. When you finish maybe about two games here in Tokyo, then you might be ready to work on a longer leash.' But then suddenly after *FFVII* ships, he calls me over, 'Well, the *Parasite Eve* team in LA, they're running into a little difficulty, and they'd like some help.' And therein was – I wouldn't quite say it was a lie, but the 'help' part and the 'little' part of the difficulty were very, very untrue.

On the excitement of working on *FFVII*:

I've never had any kind of experience like I had at Square ever since. That was very unique, and it essentially allowed me to grow to a point where I was able to create my own company, and work on things that I wanted to work on. It'd be nice if more people were [given that kind of chance].

As Square built its new US headquarters in 1996, Kyoko Higo was one of the first people hired in the marketing department. She went on to head up the company's US public relations efforts before leaving in 2004.

On how she got hired at Square:

How did I get there? By chance. I was not in games at that time. Square-soft Inc., the US office, had just opened in 1996 ... That was in Costa Mesa, Orange County. And I was actually a corporate paralegal at the American headquarters of Honda, which is in Torrance [nearby] ...

[Squaresoft US] happened to be looking for a bilingual in-house counsel and a bilingual paralegal. And, by chance, the folks who had placed me at Honda's legal division ... they asked me if I was interested in interviewing for this Japanese videogame company that was starting and had this reputation of producing great games, and now they're coming to America and they want to set this office up the right way. And they were just desperately looking for a lot of bilinguals in a variety of positions.

So I said, 'OK, I'll go check them out.' At that time, I was interested in something in a little bit of a more fast-paced industry. The automotive industry was a little too slow, especially in the legal field. So I was curious enough to take that interview. And I walked in, interviewed. By the time I left, I already had this feeling they needed someone like myself also in the marketing and PR department. Because they had no one in marketing, PR, creative services. Nothing like that. So when I got the callback, they asked me if I was interested in interviewing for the second time, but this time it would not be for the paralegal position, and that I would be a marketing assistant.

My gut feeling was like, 'OK, well I'm on this path to a legal career. Why would I do this?' But something about the, I guess, potential and charm of working for [a company that] was maybe closer to me in terms of the generation of what we grew up with [appealed to me] ... And so, it was a major decision for me because that meant I was putting my legal career path on hold, and going into a discipline that I had really no formal education, training or background in. But I ended up taking the job.

On working two jobs on *Final Fantasy VII*:

[My job] was really in the marketing department, but [I also helped] as the QA translator, essentially translating bugs pretty much every night. As soon as the QA team closed out their day of reporting all the bugs, around 5 or 6 p.m. at that time, myself and the QA manager, Jonathan Williams, we would sort of take a break, and either go get a light snack or something, and regroup at this one little round table in our office. And he would literally bring out a printed stack, like the thickness of an encyclopedia. 'Here's today's bugs.' And with a pen or pencil in hand, we would go over every single bug, and mark it 'A', 'B', or 'C'. Whatever came out as 'A' had to be translated ASAP. And 'B' if we get to it ... I forget what the cut-off was.

Basically after we'd go through this thick bug report, that would be 9 or 10 p.m. I'd go back to my desk and start translating every 'A' bug into a text format, because there was no bug database at that time. And so it's literally a brand new text file every single night. And there were two other marketing assistants who were hired around the same time, and we all happened to be bilingual ... So the three of us would go back to our desks, and [we would translate for] however many hours it took. Most of the time, easily a couple hours. We would send off the text file, the bug report, and then come back in the morning as marketing assistants. So the phrase that we were using was, 'We have two jobs.' One was the 9 to 5 marketing assistant job. And then like an after-hours shift, which was a QA translator.

On the first day on the job:

I remember the day I walked in. I walked in and we had an office manager, and you know there was a bit of an orientation, like meeting everyone, most of [whom] I'd already met during the interview. I get set up, and I just remember the very first assignment that I got was this manila folder – the folded folder – that said 'website' ... The company had just registered squaresoft.com, but it had that 'under construction' icon going and there was nothing live. So that was my day one.

On promoting *Final Fantasy: The Spirits Within*:

That same year, whether it was a good or bad thing, it was *Final Fantasy* the movie but also *Tomb Raider* the movie. There were two big video game franchises going to film. So it was almost like, even if Columbia Pictures or our side didn't want to be compared to or bucketed into this [comparison], we really had no choice.

On bringing a *Final Fantasy* concert to the US:

I was able to fulfil a tiny sort of dream that I had while working at Square, and that was to bring the *Final Fantasy* concert to the US. And the very first one we did in 2004, the day before E3 opened, was at the Walt Disney Concert Hall. And, as geeky as this sounds, that was actually a dream come true for me. I was actually volunteering at the MOCA museum, which is right across the street, on the weekends, as just a museum volunteer, and I happened to be a huge fan of Frank Gehry, who's the architect of that concert hall. So I saw the concert hall from ground up being built, and I was like, 'Oh my gosh, one day if we could have a videogame concert in the States, then it has to be at this location.' And that was just my one kind of goal for the last year I worked at Square. And we were able to execute it, and I was pretty much in awe that it happened.

As the movie director on *Final Fantasy VII* and the co-director of *Final Fantasy: The Spirits Within*, Motonori Sakakibara arrived at Square without much experience in games, but brought a cinematic sensibility that the company had been missing.

On how he got to Square in the first place:

I started my career in '89, so I had spent already five or seven years [working in New York before I joined Square. And, I knew Kazuyuki Hashimoto from that job. So after he took a job at Square] he was looking for somebody who was interested in joining from the 3D world. And at the same time, my company, they shut down the studio. So I was looking for a job, and Kazu called me, saying, 'How about joining Square?'

On working with Yoshinori Kitase:

He loves movies. I believe that he loves gaming, but at the same level he loves *Star Wars* and movies. So I always could understand what his vision was for cinematics and cutscenes – what kind of camera was cool for what shot. [His ideas tended to come from a cinematic point of view rather than just what worked for the gameplay.] So that was kind of a surprise. Because I'd worked with lots of movie people, but I'd never worked with gaming people. So I was curious how much they understood the literacy of movies, but Kitase-san had a very good sensibility.

On working with Nobuo Uematsu:

I didn't work closely with him, because music was kind of post-production from our point of view. But he is very talented, and he is a genius musician. One thing is, at the end of the [*Final Fantasy VII*], everyone was working very seriously to make the deadline, right? And I remember – I don't know which scenes, but I changed some of the editing – and he was mad. [Laughs] Because he was trying to match [his music to] the movies, and then I changed the timing.

On working with *FFVII* lead programmer Ken Narita:

He was very special because he was very open-minded and he was funny. A funny programmer is very rare. Usually, a programmer just works on the computer and doesn't talk a lot, but Narita-san was always making fun of people and creating a good mood for the team, which is unusual.

On why *The Spirits Within* flopped:

It was too early. I was in Los Angeles at that point and there were lots of billboards on the highway, but nobody knew who the actor and actress were. Most people were looking for a star in the theatre, but there was no star ... These characters were so realistic that people saw them as real humans on the poster, but they didn't know who they were.

On what he would change if remaking *The Spirits Within*:

I think I would make the story better. 'Better' meaning – the theme was very strong and clear, but how to cook the story, right? And how to visualise the story, and create more attractive character designs. Especially the main character ... At that point, we were always challenging ourselves to make a realistic human appearance, and we created realistic human skin, right? But in other movies in theatres, actresses have some treatment on their skin. That's very common. So, because we went for realistic skin, the actress looks like she doesn't have any treatment. So it should be more realistic like an actress, not like a normal person. So there's lots of stuff we could do if we did it again.

On his post-Square company, Sprite Animation:

We established this company in 2002 with about 10 people from Square USA. We started the company to create original movies or TV shows for the US market. And we spent two years in Hawaii, and then moved to here, LA, in 2004. We created some demo reels and pitched to Cartoon Network and Disney, companies like that.

Final Fantasy VII's graphics got the lion's share of the headlines, but its music took the game's cinematic quality to another level – and, to many, holds up better years later. Nobuo Uematsu led that effort.

On what he remembers most about *Final Fantasy VII*'s music:

The visuals were changing dramatically, so I felt that the kind of music I did up through *Final Fantasy VI* wouldn't match the game any more. I needed to do something new.

On online reports that he spent two years working on *FFVI* and less than one year on *FFVII*:

Some information might have gotten mixed up there. I don't remember spending two years working on *FFVI*. Usually, I would ask for at least eight months to work on a title. If it was a PlayStation title, I would usually end up spending at least a year. For *FFVI*, I don't remember exactly how many months, but it couldn't have been over a year.

On the biggest challenge working on *FFVII*:

Basically, since *Final Fantasy I*, I had been constantly creating the music for the series. So just because I was working on a PlayStation title, that didn't really change my approach too much. I was always trying to bring out the most I could on each game. However, the number of sounds I was able to use at one time [increased a lot] ... Also, since the visuals were more clear and impressive, I also thought that the kind of music that would go with the visuals was the kind of music that would go with movies. That was a bit of a change in my approach.

On working with Hironobu Sakaguchi:

Obviously, we've worked together for a long, long, long time, and I don't think he's changed at all since I first met him. He always has a super-clear vision of what he wants to do, and he structures his plans perfectly. His job is to deliver his plans to his people so they can execute them. But, when he faces any problems, he's quick to change plans to finish the game without even hesitating. His footwork is really light, which is great.

Sakaguchi also wanted to become a musician. So he knows a lot about music and loves music. And so when I first worked with him on *FFI*, he had super detailed directions and was super hands-on. But over time, he's loosened up a lot to the point where he will just hand over the scenario and be like, 'OK, compose the tracks.' We've definitely built up a trust over time. That said, he's always super hands-on and detailed with the first track I hand in.

This actually happened recently. I sent over three tracks [for the mobile role-playing game *Terra Battle*], and Sakaguchi wrote a super-long email back saying, 'OK this is what I don't like about this track,' and blah, blah, blah. Super-detailed comments. And he said, 'And therefore, I want you to redo all three tracks.' Of course, for a moment that pisses you off. But I'm OK with that because I know how much Sakaguchi understands music and I can see the passion behind it when he sends an email that long. So, because of that, I like working with him.

On working with Yoshinori Kitase on *FFVII*:

During *Final Fantasy V*, [Kitase] was working in an assistant role. I'm kind of his sempai – I was in a higher position, so my perception of him was that he was always kind of the assistant. I didn't realise he was in the director role on *FFVII*. It just seemed like the young kid was trying very hard and doing his job.

On working with Tetsuya Nomura on *FFVII*:

Yeah, kind of a similar thing [to Kitase]. Nomura is from Kochi, and so am I. And so was the president during that time. So a lot of people from Kochi were [working on *Final Fantasy* in those days].

In 2016, guest interviewer James Mielke met *Final Fantasy VII* character and battle visual director Tetsuya Nomura in a Tokyo cafe. They were there to film Nomura sketching *FFVII*'s protagonist Cloud Strife, but they also spoke briefly about Nomura's roots, Cloud as a character and Nomura's penchant for zips. Unfortunately, they didn't have the right pencil on hand for the sketch ...

Tetsuya Nomura

This isn't a mechanical pencil. It's hard to draw with and I can't get all the details, so this is going to be really rough.

James Mielke

What manga artist had the biggest influence on you growing up?

Tetsuya Nomura

I left Kochi-ken [a prefecture of Japan located on the south coast of Shi-koku] and I came to Tokyo wanting to be a manga artist, so I had a lot of artists that I liked. Kamijo Atsushi had the biggest influence on me. I liked him so much I even submitted a comment to him through a magazine.

James Mielke
What did he work on?

Tetsuya Nomura
You probably don't know him. He did *To-Y* and *Mob Hunter*. They're not very famous.

James Mielke
So, your goal wasn't to work in games, but to work in manga?

Tetsuya Nomura
Yeah, I really wanted to work on manga ... I want to redraw this [sketch of Cloud] ... [Laughs] I need a mechanical pencil. It's awkward.

James Mielke
There's a gift shop across the street. I'll go get one.

Tetsuya Nomura
No, no. It's OK.

James Mielke
A manga artist has tight deadlines and has to work under a lot of pressure, but at Square Enix it seems like there's more flexibility. Do you think it worked out for the best?

Tetsuya Nomura
Yeah, a manga artist has to do all their work alone and under tight deadlines. Your output is the limit to your achievement. Not only do I have more time to work on character designs with my current job, I work with a lot of artists, so I can draw on a bigger scale ... What's the date today?

James Mielke
September 18.

Tetsuya Nomura
Here. [Finishes drawing of Cloud.]

James Mielke
Who gave Cloud his name?

Tetsuya Nomura
I did.

James Mielke
What were you thinking about when designing him?

Tetsuya Nomura
His look has evolved over the years because he's appeared in so many different games, and he's become more of what fans think of him. Today he's more a symbol of heroism. But, originally I didn't want to create a heroic character. I wanted to make a more human, weak character with flaws. I wanted him to be a character with feelings, a heart, and someone who could be more human. I named him Cloud, as in overcast grey clouds, because he was a slightly depressed, moody character.

James Mielke
Do you think your version of Cloud has changed over the years?

Tetsuya Nomura
I've drawn Cloud the most over the years. I've had the most practice with him so he's the easiest to draw ... Sometimes I feel like I want to change him, but people are so used to seeing him a certain way at this point that it's hard to do that.

James Mielke
When people think of you, they think of zippers and chains.

Tetsuya Nomura
There was a time when I made a point of wearing a lot of zippers because I heard people say that. But I lost interest and don't wear them as much anymore. Only where necessary. This [one I'm wearing now] is for practical purposes.

James Mielke
I wish I had a chain when I had lost my wallet in Shinjuku earlier this week. I got the wallet back, but they took the money.

Tetsuya Nomura
See, if you had a chain, you wouldn't have lost your money. If you have this many chains on your belt [points to his wallet] you're not going to lose it.

James Mielke
But it's a hassle at the airport.

Tetsuya Nomura
I just pack it in my carry on.

James Mielke
Is there a character you feel like you put too many zippers on and wish you had dialled it back?

Tetsuya Nomura
There are probably too many. [Laughs] That's just the way I am. If people point something out, I'm going to counter it and double down. Not only with zippers; that's just how I deal with that sort of thing.

As head of Square in the US, Yoshihiro Maruyama led the company during the creation of a new office in Costa Mesa, California, and the release of *Final Fantasy VII*. Later, he moved on to high profile positions elsewhere – notably, head of Microsoft's Xbox division in Japan.

On how he got hired at Square:

[I worked at management consulting firm] McKinsey & Company from '93 to '95. And during that time my boss, Ken Ohmae, he was kind of a Japanese management guru. We went to meet Mr Yamauchi of Nintendo sometime in '94, and he introduced both Mr Ohmae and myself to Square – at the time, *Final Fantasy* was a big franchise for the Super Nintendo. So I met the president and also the founding owner of Squaresoft, Mr Miyamoto ...

After two years working for Ken Ohmae, I was thinking of moving into a different industry, and then the president of Squaresoft invited me to join the company, because Square was thinking of expanding their overseas business, particularly US business, at the time. So that's how I was hired – because I was involved in management consulting and I wanted to work for the overseas operation of a Japanese company.

On working with Square executives in Japan:

I never worked with Miyamoto, because he was a major shareholder of the company but he was not CEO. Mr Mizuno was very hands-off. He wanted to let people manage their operations independently. But Mr Takechi was very hands-on.

On running the US branch of a Japanese company:

I flew to Japan quite often in those days. [They didn't like working] just by phone or by email. They also requested me to be there in person. Many Japanese companies, you know, they tend to control from Tokyo ...

[There were a lot of disagreements between the US and Japanese offices,] but the general direction of the management was already decided, so minor disagreements always happen, but that's how it worked.

On why *FFVII* was such a success:

The reason why it was successful was mainly because of the transition from 2D to 3D, and lots of pretty graphics with 3D characters. Also, the story was very compelling. And also, Nomura's characters – almost all those characters were designed by Tetsuya Nomura – those characters were very powerful. So it's a combination of amazing graphics with very strong characters and very good gameplay throughout. *Final Fantasy IV, V, VI* – they were all great. But *VII* was equally good with amazing graphics and with stronger characters.

On Tetsuya Nomura pitching *Kingdom Hearts*:

I worked very closely with Nomura because, while he was pitching the *Kingdom Hearts* games to Disney, I was at [Square's Costa Mesa office nearby]. So I used to go and visit the Disney Interactive office often with Nomura. And when he started pitching the *Kingdom Hearts* concept, initially Disney [staff] were really surprised that he was combining Square characters with Disney characters, and they were concerned. But his efforts paid off ... His concept kept changing during his pitch to Disney, but ... his creative pitch was very strong.

On a lesser-known Square/Disney collaboration:

[In 2000, I left my role at Square US and] started a joint venture with Disney, D Wonderland. It was the Miyamoto project. Miyamoto wanted to have a joint venture with Disney, to make an online Disney game destination [for kids]. I think the idea was maybe 10 years too early, so it didn't go well ... I was there for two years, then the operation kind of wound down. Then I went to work for Microsoft.

Biographies

D

Yoshitaka Amano
Image illustrator, freelance

Perhaps the most famous *Final Fantasy* team member to never work at Square, Yoshitaka Amano started his career in the '60s as an illustrator working on anime such as *Speed Racer*, but went freelance in the '80s and has worked for himself ever since. He was involved with the *Final Fantasy* series from the beginning, handling much of the early promotional artwork, and stuck with the series on a freelance basis as time went on.

Chris Ansell
Project manager, Sony Computer Entertainment Europe

Starting in Sony Computer Entertainment's Australian office, Chris Ansell soon made his way to Sony Computer Entertainment Europe, where he helped with the European release of *Final Fantasy VII*. He later went on to marketing roles with Blizzard, Radical Entertainment, ZeniMax Online Studios and others. In 2014, he started his own marketing consultancy: Ansell Creative Group.

David Bamberger
Senior product manager, Sony Computer Entertainment America

Spending his career in marketing, David Bamberger has worked with many of the largest companies in the game industry – from Electronic Arts to Ubisoft to Eidos. While at Sony, he worked on the rollout plans for *Final Fantasy VII*'s North American release, coordinating with Square's US office on packaging, advertising and merchandise. In 2009, he joined Sega, working out of its San Francisco office.

Keith Boesky
President, Eidos (1997-1999)

Starting his career as an attorney, Keith Boesky served as the president of Eidos at the time Square was looking for a publishing partner for a PC version of *Final Fantasy VII*. After leaving Eidos, he became an agent with ICM, and later he went on to start his own consulting company, taking a variety of advisory and board member positions in and around the game industry.

Gloria Broadbent
Project manager and Spanish translator, SDL

In the mid-'90s, Gloria Broadbent took a job with translation agency SDL, which Sony frequently hired to localise its games for release in different territories. While there, she oversaw SDL's work on *Final Fantasy VII* – which it translated into French, German and Spanish – and personally spent a lot of time translating the game's poetry into Spanish. In 2010, she left SDL to join Alfresco, doing translation work on non-game projects.

William Chen
Lead programmer, Square US (1997-2000)

Early in his career, William Chen joined Square's Costa Mesa office to work on the PC port of *Final Fantasy VII*, and stayed there for a few years. After he left, he took engineering roles at LucasArts, The Collective, Activision, Disney Interactive and Electronic Arts before moving to China to work on a variety of mobile and virtual reality projects.

Hiroki Chiba
Event planner, Square Japan

A longtime employee of Square, Hiroki Chiba joined the company in 1993, played a small role on *Final Fantasy VII* working on the game's Gold Saucer amusement park and the character Vincent, and went on to contribute to many of Square's *Final Fantasy* games over the years that followed. Most notably, he served as the director of 2016's *World of Final Fantasy*, a game designed to appeal more to younger players than the series' mainline sequels.

Elaine Di Iorio
Manager of business development, Square US

In 1996, Elaine Di Iorio joined Square's Costa Mesa office as employee number 13, working for executive vice president Yoshihiro Maruyama. Over the course of four years there, she handled many of the company's business relationships with Sony Computer Entertainment America and Europe, as well as strategy guide publisher BradyGames. She also played a role in setting up Square's deal with Eidos to port, market and distribute *Final Fantasy VII* on PC, and stuck around for a couple of years after the port's release to work on a variety of games. After leaving Square, she went on to business development roles at studios Blizzard and Red 5, as well as others outside the game industry.

Steve Gray
Vice president of game production, Square USA

Arriving at Square with a background in CG production, Steve Gray was one of the top figures in the company's Marina del Rey office and primarily spent his time there overseeing the game *Parasite Eve*. After a falling out with some higher ups, he ended up leaving just before the team finished the game, and thus his name didn't end up in the credits. Following his time at Square, Gray went on to start independent studio Heavy Iron Studios, went to EA to work on *Lord of the Rings* games, and spent almost 10 years at Tencent, among other jobs.

George Harrison
Senior vice president, marketing and communications, Nintendo of America (1992–2007)

One of Nintendo's most visible marketing figures, George Harrison worked for General Mills, Pepsi and Quaker Oats before joining Nintendo in 1992. At Nintendo, he oversaw the company's US marketing efforts up through the launch of the Wii. After leaving Nintendo, he went on to run the consulting firm Harrison Insights.

Kazuyuki Hashimoto
CG supervisor, Square Japan; Chief technical officer and senior vice president, Square USA

One of the key figures behind *Final Fantasy VII*'s tech, Kazuyuki Hashimoto joined Square in 1995 with a background in 3D graphics from computer manufacturer Symbolics. At Square, he set up a new graphics pipeline and hired a team of engineers, initially working on the *Final Fantasy VI: The Interactive CG Game* tech demo. After finishing his work on that and *FFVII*, he played a similar role in building a pipeline and team for Square's Honolulu studio, working on the movie *Final Fantasy: The Spirits Within*, then left the company once the Honolulu studio closed.

Kyoko Higo
Assistant marketing associate, Square US

Starting her career in Honda's legal department, Kyoko Higo soon joined Square's US office as a marketing assistant and, on the side, also served as a quality assurance translator. On *Final Fantasy VII*, that meant pulling a nightly after-hours shift to organise and translate bugs found in the California office and send them back to the development team in Tokyo. In 2004, she left Square and joined startup publisher XSEED alongside a handful of former Square co-workers. Then, in 2006, she went freelance, working as a consultant, interpreter and business development manager with many of the biggest game companies in Japan.

Frank Hom
Associate producer, Eidos (1995–2001)

Serving as the main point of contact at Eidos, Frank Hom oversaw development of the *Final Fantasy VII* PC port, working closely with the development team in Square's Costa Mesa office. As the PC version ran into delays, he essentially became a middleman between the developers at Square and the executives at Eidos. Hom left Eidos in 2001 and spent nine years as a producer at Ubisoft before joining Sega of America in 2010.

Rex Ishibashi
Vice president of business development, Electronic Arts (1997–2001)

Starting his career as a consultant out of college, Rex Ishibashi got to know some of the higher ups at Electronic Arts as clients, then took a variety of jobs at companies including 3DO and Wired magazine. In 1997 he joined EA and, while there, helped manage its publishing partnership with Square. He left after a few years and took a number of jobs in and out of the game industry, one of which saw him return to EA to serve as general manager and president of EA Japan. In 2013, he founded Originator, a game studio built to make mobile apps for kids.

Jun Iwasaki
Vice president of marketing, Square US

As the head of Western marketing for *Final Fantasy VII*, Jun Iwasaki worked closely with Sony and ad agencies to promote the game to an audience unfamiliar with role-playing games. Following *FFVII*'s release, he took over as president of Square's US office, then left in 2004 after a disagreement with then-president and CEO of Square Enix, Yoichi Wada. Iwasaki says his main regret upon leaving was that he wasn't able to see through a marketing campaign for *Dragon Quest* 7 in the West; he had developed a plan to pit *Final Fantasy* and *Dragon Quest* fans against each other, since the games took different approaches to the role-playing genre and were under the same roof after Square merged with Enix. After leaving Square, Iwasaki started XSEED, a small publisher that releases Japanese games in the West. And, in 2012, he took over GungHo Online Entertainment America, the US branch of the company behind Japanese mobile sensation *Puzzle & Dragons*.

Michael Jones
Engineering director, Silicon Graphics (1992–1999)

One of the higher-ups at Silicon Graphics in the '90s, Michael Jones oversaw products such as 3D graphics language OpenGL, and was one of the first people outside of Square to see the company's experiments in taking *Final Fantasy* into 3D. He went on to become a chief technology advocate at Google and CEO of VR glasses company Wearality, among other jobs.

Shinichiro Kajitani
Vice president, Square USA

One of Square's first employees, Shinichiro Kajitani joined the team in 1986 on the same day as Nasir Gebelli, the programmer of the first three *Final Fantasy* games. Initially, Kajitani bounced between different roles, starting in sales, then dabbling in programming and production management. In the early '90s he helped Square with recruiting, and oversaw administrative purchases for the company, later joining Square USA and sitting on the Square EA board. After leaving Square in 2002, he joined game publisher Capcom, then went to development studio Game Republic, and then to tech powerhouse (and occasional game developer) Silicon Studio.

Hiroshi Kawai
Character programmer, Square Japan

An MIT graduate, Hiroshi Kawai initially interviewed with Square to be a translator, hoping to get his foot in the door. Square hired him as a game designer instead, and then he quickly shifted over to what he really wanted to do: programming. At that point, he started dabbling in early Nintendo 64 and PlayStation hardware research and helping with the *Final Fantasy VI: The Interactive CG Game* tech demo. He went on to work as a programmer on *Final Fantasy VII*, then later became a lead programmer on *Final Fantasy IX*. In the early 2000s, he left Square to join Microsoft and worked as a producer and lead programmer on a variety of games, including *Lost Odyssey*. Following that, he started his own programming studio, In Control, to work on various projects outside the game industry.

Yoshinori Kitase
Director, Square Japan

With *Final Fantasy VI*, Yoshinori Kitase took over as the series' director. And when *Final Fantasy VII* came around, he fell into the same role. Team members describe Kitase as calmer and quieter than many high-profile game directors, and say that his cinematic sensibilities played a big role in shaping *FFVII*'s CG cutscenes. In the years following *FFVII*'s release, Kitase stayed at Square, directing and producing many of the biggest *Final Fantasy* games.

Seth Luisi
Associate producer, Sony Computer Entertainment America

Working at Sony for more than 15 years, Seth Luisi helped produce dozens of games for the US market, *Final Fantasy VII* among them. He's best known for coming up with the idea for, and overseeing, the *SOCOM* military shooter series, which went on to sell more than 10 million units.

Shigeo Maruyama
Chairman, Sony Computer Entertainment

The original PlayStation boss, Shigeo Maruyama had a long career in the music industry before moving into games. In the early '90s, he shifted from his role as Sony Music's CEO to help get PlayStation off the ground, going on to serve as the chairman of Sony Computer Entertainment. After approximately 10 years working on PlayStation, he returned to the music industry.

Yoshihiro Maruyama
Executive vice president, Square US

In the early '90s, Yoshihiro Maruyama worked for Japanese management guru Ken Ohmae, who had a variety of contacts in the game industry. And, at one point in 1994, Ohmae took Maruyama to meet with former Nintendo president Hiroshi Yamauchi, who in turn introduced both of them to Square's top executives. A year later, Square hired Maruyama to run the company's US headquarters. As the head of the Costa Mesa, California office, he oversaw *FFVII*'s Western release and signed deals to release the game on PC in the US, Europe and Korea. In 2003, Maruyama took over Microsoft's Xbox division in Japan. Following that, he went on to work as an agent, setting up deals such as connecting high-profile Japanese writer/director Yasumi Matsuno with independent studio Playdek for the role-playing game *Unsung Story*.

Yusuke Naora
Art director, Square Japan

When starting at Square in the early '90s, Yusuke Naora began work on *Final Fantasy VI* without ever having played a role-playing game. A couple of years later he took on the role of *Final Fantasy VII*'s art director, and he then stayed with Square for two decades, working on a large variety of games. In 2016, he finished his work as one of a team of art directors on *Final Fantasy XV*, overseeing the creation of the game's characters, then left the company.

Kazushige Nojima
Scenario writer, Square Japan

In the late '90s and early 2000s, Kazushige Nojima wrote the stories for many of Square's biggest games, *Final Fantasy VII* among them. Yet, when growing up, he says he was a bigger fan of Enix's

Dragon Quest than he was of *Final Fantasy*, considering *Dragon Quest II* and *III* to be 'the quintessential Japanese RPGs'. That doesn't mean he would want to try his hand at the *Dragon Quest* series, though. 'I couldn't do it,' he says. 'I just regard it so highly. I met Yuji Horii, who created *Dragon Quest*, when Square and Enix merged and I was just so tense. I couldn't say anything. It was a profound experience.' Nojima left Square in 2003 to go freelance, though still worked regularly with Square Enix.

Tetsuya Nomura
Character and battle visual director, Square Japan

One of Square's longest-running character designers, Tetsuya Nomura started with the *Final Fantasy* series as a tester on *Final Fantasy IV* and went on to contribute to the series in various forms in the years following, often taking on high-profile director and producer roles. He also branched out into many of Square's other games, most notably overseeing the creation and development of the action role-playing franchise *Kingdom Hearts*.

Veronique Raguet
French translator, SDL

Working at translation agency SDL, Veronique Raguet was part of the team that localised *Final Fantasy VII* into French. She dabbled in a handful of different games at the time, but then moved on to a series of non-game translation jobs at companies such as Telelingua France and Hewlett Packard.

John Riccitiello
President and chief operating officer, Electronic Arts (1998–2004)

One of the game industry's long-standing executives, John Riccitiello worked at Clorox, Pepsi and Sara Lee, among others, before making his way to Electronic Arts in the late '90s. While at EA, he saw the success of *Final Fantasy VII* and struck a deal with Square to publish Square's games in the US. He later left and then re-joined EA before going on to take the role of CEO of game engine provider Unity.

Hironobu Sakaguchi
Producer and executive vice president, Square Japan; Chairman and chief executive officer, Square USA

The creator of the *Final Fantasy* series, Hironobu Sakaguchi became Square's first industry celebrity. Many credit him with not only keeping Square from going under in the late '80s, but also with being ahead of the curve by moving *Final Fantasy* into 3D, online play and the film industry. After completing the film *Final Fantasy: The Spirits Within*, he left Square and founded production studio Mistwalker.

Motonori Sakakibara
Movie director, Square Japan

As Square began hiring staff in the mid-'90s to make high-end computer graphics, Motonori Sakakibara joined the team, first working on the *Final Fantasy VI: The Interactive CG Game* tech demo, then overseeing *Final Fantasy VII*'s cutscenes. He went on to co-direct Square's movie *Final Fantasy: The Spirits Within* and then started a CG animation company called Sprite Animation with a team of about 10 people who had worked on *The Spirits Within*.

Alexander O. Smith
Localisation specialist, Square US and Japan (1998–2002)

Growing up fan of Apple II and Mac games rather than Japanese RPGs, Alexander O. Smith joined Square shortly after *Final Fantasy VII*'s release and gained a reputation among fans as one of the best writers in localisation for his work on games like *Vagrant Story* and *Final Fantasy X*. Following *Final Fantasy X*, Smith left Square to pursue a freelance career, though continued to work with Square on a project-by-project basis.

Darren Smith
Project manager/manager, Nintendo of America (1993–2000)

Joining Nintendo out of college, Darren Smith worked on a variety of behind-the-scenes projects, such as the Gateway system that allowed people to play Nintendo games on aeroplanes and in hotel rooms. In 1993, he became Nintendo's representative at Silicon Graphics, helping coordinate plans for the Nintendo 64 hardware. After that, he went on to take a variety of jobs, some at Nintendo, some as a consultant and some running his own studios.

Tomoyuki Takechi
President and chief executive officer, Square

In 1990, while working at Shikoku Bank, Tomoyuki Takechi started working with Square to help manage its finances. That led to him helping Square go public in 1994, and then joining the company in 1996 – right when Square was deciding whether to make *Final Fantasy VII* for Nintendo or Sony hardware.

As president and chief executive officer at Square, he led negotiations with Sony for Square to publish *FFVII* for the PlayStation. In 2000, he became Square's chairman, and in 2001 he left to take responsibility for the company taking a financial loss. Following his time at Square, he went on to work as president of development studio AQ Interactive and to serve on the boards of various companies in and related to the game industry.

Nobuo Uematsu
Music composer, Square Japan

One of Square's first employees, Nobuo Uematsu made a name for himself as the composer of the early *Final Fantasy* games and stuck with the franchise for more than 20 years, contributing less as time went on. *Final Fantasy VII* marked his first game on PlayStation, which gave him more storage space to work with, though he hesitated to use it all since he didn't want to add to the game's load times. In 2004, Uematsu left Square to go freelance.

Yoichi Wada
President and chief executive officer, Square/ Square Enix (2001–2013)

A few years after *Final Fantasy VII*'s launch, Yoichi Wada stepped in to take over Square's operations. Some on the team disagreed with his approach of putting more formal processes in place, lining up multiple *Final Fantasy* spin-off games, merging with Enix and acquiring Taito, Eidos and others. But Wada held his role until 2013, when he stepped down to form experimental cloud-gaming team Shinra Technologies, which Square initially funded. Wada remained with Square in a reduced capacity as chairman of the board of the company's Tokyo subsidiary for two years, then left to focus on Shinra, which went under in 2016. Following Shinra's demise, Wada became an advisor to a variety of companies in the game industry.

Junichi Yanagihara
Executive vice president, Square USA

A former lawyer in Seattle, Junichi Yanagihara helped Square establish three offices over the course of the '90s. He started with Square's first US headquarters in Redmond, Washington, then helped open its studios in Los Angeles and Honolulu. Yanagihara stayed with the Honolulu studio until its final day in 2002, tying up the remaining legal issues, then branched out with a team of former co-workers to start independent CG animation studio Sprite Animation.

Shuhei Yoshida
Square account manager, Sony Computer Entertainment

A popular figure at Sony, Shuhei Yoshida worked his way up through the company. In the early years, he had a hand in producing some of Sony's biggest first-party hits, from *Crash Bandicoot* to *Gran Turismo*. Then he worked on the third-party support team at the time *Final Fantasy VII* came along. Eventually, he moved up to oversee all of Sony's first-party titles.

Tatsuya Yoshinari
Programmer, Square Japan

As a student, Tatsuya Yoshinari was such a fan of the early *Final Fantasy* titles that he made his own role-playing game and sent it to Square. Someone at the company liked it enough to offer him a job, and in 1995 he started as a programmer on the Super Famicom board game *Koi wa Balance*. Next he joined the *Final Fantasy VII* team, working on the motorcycle chase and roller coaster minigames, then moved on to Square's action RPG *Parasite Eve* and *Final Fantasy IX*. After that, he left to join Microsoft and assisted on titles such as RPG *Lost Odyssey*.

Index

E

Colophon

F

Colophon

First published in the UK in 2018 by Read-Only
Memory, an imprint of Thames & Hudson

This edition published in the United Kingdom
in 2023 by Thames & Hudson Ltd,
181A High Holborn, London WC1V 7QX

First published in the United States of America
in 2023 by Thames & Hudson Inc.,
500 Fifth Avenue, New York, New York 10110

500 Years Later:
An Oral History of Final Fantasy VII
© 2023 Thames & Hudson Ltd, London

Foreword © 2023 James Chen
Text © 2023 Matt Leone
Illustrations © 2023 sparrows

Designed by Rachel Dalton

British Library Cataloguing-in-Publication Data
A catalogue record for this book is available
from the British Library

Library of Congress Control Number
2023936975

ISBN 978-0-500-02736-3

Printed in China by Shenzhen Reliance Printing Co. Ltd.

MIX
Paper from
responsible sources
FSC® C102842
FSC
www.fsc.org

The author would like to thank: Kainaz Amaria,
Clayton Ashley, Jonathan Castillo, Forbes
Conrad, Allegra Frank, Chris Grant, Alex
Highsmith, Brittany Holloway-Brown, Emily
Leone, Tracy Pon Leone, Tara Long, Sara
Masetti, Samantha Mason, Michael McWhertor,
James Mielke, Joy Mielke, Hiroko Minamoto,
James Mountain, Scott Nelson, CJ Nichols,
Ashley Oh, Jeff Ramos, Lindley Sico, Kavya
Sukumar, and Irwin Wong.

The publishers would like to thank: Matt Leone,
Chris Grant, Samantha Mason, Lindley Sico,
Tara Long, Clayton Ashley, Camilla Smallwood,
Silvia Novak, and Peter Chuckles.

This book is an independent history of *Final
Fantasy VII*, and is not endorsed, sponsored,
or authorised by Square Enix Co., Ltd or any
videogame companies.

Adapted from *Final Fantasy VII: An Oral
History*, Copyright © 2017 by Vox Media, Inc.
Originally published on Polygon.com, January
9, 2017.

polygon.com/a/final-fantasy-7